TAMING OUR MONKEY MIND

TAMING OUR MONKEY MIND

Insight, Detachment, Identity

Phyllis Krystal

SAMUEL WEISER, INC.

York Beach, Maine

First published in 1994 by
Samuel Weiser, Inc.
Box 612
York Beach, ME 03910

Library of Congress Cataloging-in-Publication Data
Krystal, Phyllis
    Taming our monkey mind : insight, detachment,
identity / by Phyllis Krystal.
        p.   cm.
    1. Sathya Sai Baba, 1926–   . 2. Spiritual life—
Hinduism.
BL1175.S385K798   1994
294.5'44—dc20   93-42842
                                                              CIP

ISBN 0-87728-793-7
CCP

Typeset in 11 point Palatino

Printed in the United States of America
99 98 97 96 95 94
10 9 8 7 6 5 4 3 2 1

The paper used in this publication meets the minimum
requirements of the American National Standard for
Permanence of Paper for Printed Library Materials
Z39.49–1984.

I dedicate this book to Sri Sathya Sai Baba who announced that I was writing it before I had given any thought to writing another book and materialized a beautiful pen for me to use with the assurance that, "The book is in the pen." Here it is—thanks to Baba!

Table of Contents

Part II: How to Tame Our Monkey Mind

Poems

Preface

This book, like the three previous ones, was prompted by Sri Sathya Sai Baba in his usual enigmatic way. He only rarely gives specific or clear directions; he prefers to suggest a course of action and then lets us decide whether we wish to pursue it or choose one more to our own liking. He explains that he will always honor our free will and will never overrule either it or our karma.

I have, however, observed that in a situation where—despite every effort—someone is still unable to come to a decision concerning a particular course of action, Baba will supply sufficient information to indicate the correct solution. But he does so only when the person has really surrended his or her own will and retains no preference for a particular outcome, and can honestly say, "Thy will, not mine."

During a visit with Baba in January 1989, he told me not to run back and forth to see him but to wait until the book I had just finished writing was published, and then bring him a copy for his blessing. My husband, Sidney, with his quick mind and habitual foresight, realized that as an officer of the Sathya Sai Society of America, he would be attending the next World Conference held in India every five years and coinciding with Baba's 65th birthday at the end of November 1990. So, before I had time to respond, Sidney asked, "For your next birthday, Swami?" Baba—with a sly smile aimed at me—knowing full well how I react to huge crowds such as those assembled at his birthday, replied, "Yes, Swami would be very happy." Unlike Sidney, I did not think quickly enough to ask if he wanted us to go twice in one year, in the event that the book in question was published before our planned visit. As usual, Baba expected me to be patient and watch and wait to discover for myself the correct time to go, when that time arrived.

The book was duly published in June 1990. Meanwhile, we had decided not to attend the 65th birthday celebration. These occasions are extremely crowded and intensely busy. Consequently, Baba is able to grant very few personal interviews. Neither is he as easily visible during *darshan* as at other times of the year.

We had attended the big 50th, 55th, and 60th birthday celebrations, each of which had been progressively more crowded than the previous one. At our advanced ages we find such huge gatherings very tiring. So, when I heard that two friends were leaving at the end of June—and since Sidney preferred not to go at that time—I decided to go with them and do as Baba had asked—take him a copy of the book "as soon as it was published."

During an interview at the end of that short visit, he told me three separate times, in a very serious tone of voice and with an equally serious facial expression, that I *must* come back for his 65th birthday. So, in view of his insistence, both Sidney and I decided to attend. Over the years I have learned that Baba never says anything that does not contain a very important hint for the person to whom he is speaking. I have also learned that the meaning is usually on many levels and not merely the most obvious surface one. Although we had no idea why he was so insistent (which in itself was unusual), my own experience had taught me that I could follow his orders with complete trust, so in the middle of November, Sidney and I—along with thousands of other devotees—arrived at the ashram in time to settle in before the coming events.

It was, indeed, just as crowded as we had anticipated. And it was incredible to see those huge throngs of people who had come from so many other countries—in addition to the vast numbers from every part of India—all being housed and fed. Many of them, I was sure, had scrimped and saved to be able to afford to make the journey, whether they came by plane from overseas or from cities, towns, or small villages in India, often taking several days to reach the ashram. They had come by car, train, bus, bullock cart, and even on foot. The intense devotion so impressively demonstrated was staggering to behold and most inspiring.

Baba was, as usual, the perfect host, showering his love on the many thousands of eager devotees gathered to honor him on his birthday. For the few days of festivities, throngs of people were everywhere, and the air was electrically charged with excitement. The energy was almost tangible and allowed everyone to function adequately, even under anything but comfortable conditions. The president of India had been invited to officiate at the opening of the new museum that houses exhibits representing the many countries where there are Sai devotees, as well as the various world religions. Many meetings were regularly taking place where delegates could discuss the activities of their organizations.

An immense statue of Hanuman, the monkey god, had been erected overlooking the playing fields, and we were fortunate to be present when Baba officiated at its dedication. The plans for a new hospital to be built near the ashram were blessed by Baba in an impressive ceremony, which we also attended. Baba gave many discourses that were translated into English for the benefit of those who could not understand Telegu, the language he usually speaks.

On the day before we planned to leave the ashram to return home, we were called for an interview along with several other Westerners. Suddenly, Baba turned his attention to me, where I sat on the floor at his feet with the other visitors, and announced, "You are writing another book, Mrs. Krystal." As usual, his comments or questions always come as a complete surprise, which he thoroughly enjoys, for he delights in catching people unaware. Since I was not planning to write another book his comment left me uncertain as to how I should reply, and from the tone of his voice it was hard to determine whether he was actually asking a question or making a statement. Finally I answered, "Yes, Baba," in that same neutral tone.

He then asked, as is his habit, "What is the title?" to which I responded as I had each previous time he had asked me that question, "I never know the title, Swami." He smiled sweetly and reassured me by saying, "Swami will provide it." Then, with the familiar wave of his right hand he produced a beautiful, slim, shiny, silver pen trimmed with gold and deep blue-green enamel, saying as he did so, "The book is in the pen." He reached for a piece of paper and scribbled on it to make sure the pen was filled with ink. Then, satisfied that it was, he handed it to me. I said, "Oh thank you Baba," to which he responded with a broad smile, "Please don't mention it." This set everyone laughing, including me, for he was mimicking my accent and tone of voice.

I was surprised and delighted, as well as highly amused. Because using a computer dazzles my eyes and gives me headaches, I always write with a pen and then later type what I have written. I knew that Baba was aware of this habit, for once when I handed him a sheaf of handwritten pages from the book I was writing at the time, he referred to my penmanship as "crow's-feet scratches," which is indeed correct, for it is illegible except to me and, of course, to Baba!

Later in the interview, he told me to bring the new book to him for his blessing at the opening of the new hospital he was then planning to build. I asked when that would occur, and he answered with a knowing look, "On the day before Swami's next birthday, November 22, 1991." With no prior thought, I found myself saying, "Oh Baba, you will have to hurry to write a whole book through me in just one year," at which he laughed and replied, "Swami will."

It was not until later that I had a chance to look more carefully at the pen. As I removed the cap, I was delighted to see that it had an old-fashioned nib, like the ones I used during my youth in England. On more careful examination I discovered the word "Parker" etched on the nib, and around the gold band at the base were the words, "Made in UK." My immediate response was, "How appropriate, for I, too, was made in England," having been born there.

Over the years, Baba has produced, as if from thin air, a number of articles, such as watches and pens, bearing the name of the manufacturer or the country where they were made. Many people have cited these instances to prove that Baba is a magician and does not actually materialize these objects as he appears to do. In other words, they label him a fraud or an imposter and often lose faith in him and his teachings. But the following story may explain how Baba procures such gifts.

A man from one of the European countries was among a group of visitors called in for an interview. Baba chose to produce a gold watch with a wave of his hand. He gave it to this man, who was delighted but at the same time worried that he might not be able to take it through customs when he left India to return home. He had the presence of mind to mention his concern to Baba, who immediately agreed that there might be a problem and told the man to wait a moment. Then, to everyone's surprise, he again waved his hand in the usual circular movement and produced a bill of sale on which was printed the name of a store in the man's hometown. He handed it to the amazed man with a big smile, reassuring him with, "Now, you will have no problem."

Shortly after his return home, the man decided to pursue this incident further by paying a visit to the store listed on the bill of sale. He asked if anyone there could remember who had purchased the watch, which he showed to a salesperson who quickly replied, "That is one sale none of us will forget because the customer was so unusual. He was dressed in a long orange robe and wore his hair in a wide Afro style. But even stranger, a few minutes after he had bought the watch he returned, requesting the bill of sale, and again quickly disappeared with it."

Unlike this man, I was not able to verify the purchase of the pen, but I suspect someone in a store somewhere in England probably has a similar tale to tell. Such are the mystifying stories that circulate around Baba. He does nothing to explain such puzzling incidents, evidently preferring to allow people to come to their own conclusions. Some will doubt his veracity, while others will have even more faith in his extraordinary powers. In this way it will be as he himself expresses it, "As if a giant wind separates the chaff from the grain," the nonbelievers from the believers.

So, I now knew that I would be returning for yet another birthday the following year with a new book ready to present to Baba for his blessing. He most certainly would have to write it through me, as I had requested, for at that point I had neither the title nor the contents in mind. But I have learned to trust Baba and was certain that he would provide both the title—as he had promised—as well as the book itself, since it was "contained in the pen," as he expressed it so whimsically.

Prior to this episode I had fleetingly acknowledged to myself that probably, at some time in the future, I should write a book about the recent work I had been doing with negative thought forms. I had even jotted down a few ideas one day but quickly decided that it was premature. I had also toyed with the idea that at some future point, I should keep my promise to expand the booklet I had composed on Baba's Ceiling on Desires program, but had postponed that, too.

Interestingly enough, before I left India to return home, one morning in meditation the subject of the new book flashed into my mind, *Sathya Sai Baba and Our Monkey Mind*. So Baba had provided me with the subject, as he had promised, and so quickly. As soon as the title had emerged, the general outline began to take shape in my mind and all the pieces started to fit together into an intricate mosaic. I saw how all the isolated experiences that had occurred when we were with Baba this time had, unknown to me, pointed the way to indicate the theme of the book. And it would combine the two ideas I had so casually postponed earlier: the monkey mind and the thought-forms it spawns, together with the Ceiling on Desires program and other methods designed to train the mind to follow the example set by Hanuman, the monkey god who won freedom by serving only Rama, who represents the true Self.

I then remembered that we had been present when Baba inaugurated the new statue of Hanuman, and also that I had been asked to give a short talk to all the overseas devotees on the Ceiling on Desires program during the conference. So, without my knowledge the stage had been set for this book during our visit. I never cease to marvel at the way seemingly diverse events come together to form a clear pattern when the time is right, if only we have the patience to wait until that time and refrain from impatiently trying to force our own premature timing.

Now, I would need to watch for the right times to allow the book to flow through me, with Baba's help. In this way I could rest assured that it would be finished and ready to take to him for his blessing in November 1991, as he had requested.

Acknowledgments

First, I wish to thank Sri Sathya Sai Baba for the tremendous help and encouragement he so generously provides to those who request it and are willing to allow him to guide their lives.

I thank my daughter, Sheila, for carefully editing the manuscript as she has done with the previous ones.

I also thank Peggy Lenney for patiently and tirelessly typing the manuscript on her computer as part of her *seva*, or service, which Baba assures us all is so very important for our spiritual progress.

And last, but by no means least, I thank my husband, Sidney, for his continued support of my work, which has made it possible for me to write books and give seminars in many far-flung places.

"Your duty is to abandon. Abandon all your plans, even the best ones. Abandon all the theories you cherish, the doctrines you hold dear, the systems of knowledge that have cluttered your brain, the preferences you have accumulated, the pursuit of fame, fortune, scholarship, superiority. These are all material, objective. Enter into the objective world after becoming aware of the Atma. Then you will realize that all is the play of the Atma."

—Sri Sathya Sai Baba

PART I

IDENTIFYING
OUR MONKEY MIND

Chapter 1

Introduction

As soon as I started the actual writing, all kinds of half-forgotten experiences and memories began to surface from the past. As I watched them emerge, it became apparent that many seemingly isolated incidents in my life had prepared the way for this book. Now I needed only to bring it all into focus and share it with others.

For instance, while I was still in school in England, I discovered John Galsworthy's series of novels, *The Forsyte Saga* and the *Modern Comedy*, which I devoured as soon as I could obtain copies of the various volumes. Much as I enjoyed the books, the one that had continued to haunt me all these years was *The White Monkey*. The title was taken from a Chinese painting that was featured prominently in the story. It depicted a large white monkey with hauntingly sad brown eyes, frozen in the act of eating an orange-like fruit held in its hand, while the many rinds of the fruits it had already devoured lay strewn around it on the ground. On first seeing this painting, one of the characters in the book commented that it was "a pungent satire of life; a perfect allegory. Eat the fruits of life and discard and scatter the rinds." From the monkey's expression it appeared to be aware that there must be something more to life, and it was sad or angry because it could not reach it and would not be happy until it did. The problem was that it did not know what it was seeking. So its eyes expressed the tragedy of life incarnate.

The painting portrayed the human dilemma that Baba likens to the monkey mind that causes us to indulge our desires for satisfaction from exterior objects, only to be

trapped by them and prevented from seeking within ourselves the real and indestructible fruits; the only ones that
can give *lasting* satisfaction. It was a truly brilliant symbol
of greed. For some unknown reason, its image aroused in
my mind some hidden recognition from the past.

Many years after reading this book, while I was being
regressed into past lives, the memory of the white monkey
suddenly came to mind during one particular session. I
was observing an inner scene, which, at that time in my
present life, was completely foreign to me. It appeared to
be placed in Tibet. As I watched it unfold, I began to
identify with a young man who, I gradually compre-
hended, was a monk. Apparently he had allowed himself
to be immured in a cave high up in the mountains above
the monastery to which he belonged. This voluntary con-
finement was part of his spiritual discipline, the purpose
being to help him discover his true identity. While in the
cave he kept in telepathic contact with his Master, the High
Lama who supervised his practice from the monastery.

The exercise the teacher had given his pupil was to
observe symbols of all his desires, one at a time, and let
go of each one by squeezing out all the energy he had
deposited in them and then discarding the empty shells.
With this recognition, the old memory of the white monkey flashed into my mind and I immediately made the
connection between that representation of basic desire and
the task the monk had undertaken of ridding himself of
his desires. But, there was one big difference; whereas the
monkey was indulging his desire for the sweet succulent
fruit and discarding the empty rinds, the young lama had
elected to squeeze out all the energy contained in the symbols of his various desires until all that remained was a
pile of empty shells, leaving him free from their control
over his thoughts and therefore over his life.

Another very early memory from my present life also
fell into place. I had always wondered why this particular

one stood out so clearly from all the others and remained so vividly etched in my memory, as if I had just experienced it. I must have been about 3 or 4 years old at the time of this episode. My mother had bought a basket of big, ripe, red, and delicious-looking strawberries, which she placed in a bowl. We both sat at a table with plates in front of us, and she proceeded to give me a little lesson in unselfishness, a quality she prized very highly in others. As I was an only child she greatly feared I would become a "spoiled brat," as she expressed it frequently. So she asked me to take one strawberry from the bowl. Childlike, I took the biggest, which brought forth a stern lecture from her to the effect that I must learn to be unselfish and always let others have the best or the largest of anything. She then promptly put the big strawberry onto her own plate and told me to take a small one.

I remember well that even at that young age I was very confused by this little scene. Why, I wondered, must I always accept something inferior while others received something superior? Was it because I was bad, or not important, or did not deserve anything better? Wasn't it allowing others to be selfish while I learned to be unselfish? None of these questions was ever answered, for to ask questions or disagree with my mother was labeled impertinent; yet another sin, according to her. So I was left with the feeling of unworthiness, and the message that selfishness was a cardinal sin and unselfishness a supreme virtue.

But now that I have gained my own perspective on the whole question, I realize that my mother had the right idea. But she lacked the necessary wisdom to present it to me clearly and at an age when I would have been better able to understand it, having developed the ability to apply it without self-deprecation or a feeling of being unworthy. Now, of course, added to all the other insights, it too fits in with the theme of this book.

On looking back from my present vantage point, I am able to see that this life has given me the opportunity to learn a very hard lesson: not to become attached to what I most desired and to be willing to accept what I did not want. Now, this is a purely personal issue, since what I wanted would not necessarily be another person's preference, and those things I did not want, someone else might desire. For instance, I was not able to pursue the career I so desperately wanted, which was to become a surgeon. The only feasible alternative at that time was to train as a teacher, from which I recoiled but eventually accepted.

However, I am now convinced that it all worked out for the best and prepared me for what I am doing, though I most certainly could not have foreseen it at that time. It also gave me a preparation for understanding—to a very limited extent—Baba's teaching on nonattachment, when I eventually heard about him and his message. When I first met Baba, he materialized a ring containing a moonstone, which he instructed me to rub on the middle of my forehead whenever I had a headache in that area. This reference was reminiscent of the life in Tibet, when the young monk bashed his forehead on the stone wall of the cell in which he was living to stop the flow of images. He had been driven to this desperate act when the telepathic connection between him and his Master was broken, leaving him to complete the task he had been given to detach himself from his desires without any help.

At a later date Baba gave me an entire interview devoted to his Ceiling on Desires program, with the obvious intent that I be willing to share it by writing and speaking about the insights and experiences received by myself and others who have practiced it.

It was truly a wonderful feeling to have these separate learning experiences come together in this way and to see how this book had been initiated long before Baba gave me the pen with which to write it. Everything we have ever experienced can be used in a positive way to teach us, if we are willing to seek the lessons thus offered and learn from them. But this is not by any means an easy task, and we can succeed only if we are willing to ask Baba to help us with it.

Chapter 2

The Monkey Mind

So what exactly *is* the monkey mind? Sathya Sai Baba often refers to an individual as having a monkey mind or, in some cases, even a mad monkey mind. When I first heard him say this to someone, I wondered just what he meant by it. I could tell that it was definitely not intended as a compliment; in fact, quite the reverse. So my own restless mind immediately began trying to decipher the message contained in his remark.

Particularly in the south of India where Baba has his ashram, it is common to see groups of monkeys leaping from branch to branch in the trees they inhabit, or skittering across the ground. The females invariably carry babies hanging upside down and clinging tightly to their mothers' undersides as they run, leap, and jump. These monkeys are delightful to watch, since they are so playful, and the babies are so appealing with their big wide-open eyes observing everything. They are attracted or, more accurately, *distracted* by everything on which their glance happens to alight, especially fruit and nuts, which they relish, and shiny or brightly colored objects that arouse their curiosity. "Grab and run" appears to be their motto, for they are notorious thieves. "Yes," I thought, "it is true that people are like monkeys, easily distracted by all manner of things that keep their minds ceaselessly restless and never at peace."

To quote Baba, "Mind is very truly characterized as a monkey! Why, it is even more wayward than a monkey, for it jumps from one perch to another that is miles away in space and centuries away in time, in less time than a wink. The mind jumps from one desire to another and entangles us in its coils."

Baba often announces that he will tell a little story to illustrate a point. He always uses simple stories about familiar objects, sights, and activities from daily life to clarify his teachings, and he often quotes extracts from some of the great Indian epics such as the Ramayana, Mahabharata, and Bhagavad Gita. Here is one way he illustrates the monkey mind. "Let us examine this question, for example: Is man enslaved by external objects and the attraction they exercise over him? Or, is it some inner impulse that urges him forward to shackle himself to sorrow? I shall give an example. There are professional monkey catchers in the villages who employ a crude device for the purpose. They place in the orchards or gardens infested by the marauders a number of narrow-necked earthen pots with a handful of peanuts inside each. The monkey approaches a pot, knows that it has the delicious nuts inside, puts its long hand in and collects the nuts in its fist. Now, it finds it cannot take its arm out; the neck is too narrow for the nut-full fist! So, it sits helpless and forlorn and is easily caught and transported! It thinks that there is someone inside the pot who is holding back its arm when it tries to take it out! If only it had loosened the grip and got rid of the attachment to the nuts it could have escaped! So, too, you are victims of desire and the attachments that the desire entails. You are bound by the shackles you have yourselves fastened around you! Liberation, too, is in your hands. Contemplate the unchanging glory of God; then desire for the transient baubles of the earth will fade and you will be free."

And, another slightly different version of the same theme, also by Baba is, "Those who catch monkeys prepare a pot with a small opening in it and fill it with some sweets. The monkey who desires the food will put its hand inside the pot and take a big handful of the food. Thus, the monkey becomes unable to draw its hand out through the opening. Only on releasing its grip will the monkey be able to take its hand out. It is its desire for the food that has bound its hand. Because it took with its hand some food to fulfil its desire, it was bound there.

"This wide world is like the pot, the situations in life or in families are like the narrow top. Our desires are the sweets in the pot. The world being the pot containing the desires as sweets, man puts his hand in the pot. When he sheds his desires, he will be able to live in the world freely. To get freedom the first thing to do is to sacrifice. In philosophical terms this is called renunciation. We think that the world is binding us, but the world is lifeless. It is the desire that binds us."

These little examples give a comprehensive meaning to the term "monkey mind," and bring it right down to the essential cause, which is desire. Baba often says that if we can give up all desires we will attain enlightenment, or identification with our real Self as distinct from the physical sheath in which It resides. It is entirely a question of attachment. What do we hold on to that keeps us trapped and makes us a fair target for control by other people, ideas, things, circumstances, and a host of other attachments?

Baba tells us that we are three people. "You must learn who others think you are. They deal with you as a body, with a specific name and an identifiable form. Then you must learn about who you think you are. You are aware of your mind and its monkey tricks, its prejudices and preferences, its passions and pursuits. You are aware of an individual consciousness, of your version of 'me' and 'mine.' You must learn about the mind as an instrument that can harm you if used unwisely, or help you if used wisely. Then you have to learn about yet another you, the you you *really* are. For you are neither the body nor the mind, the intellect, the brain, the heart, or the ego. You are the Infinite Universal Absolute." The result of undertaking a task such as he suggests is true happiness, though not born of possessions or exterior circumstances but based on the security that such awareness makes possible.

So, what actually is the mind and its uses? Baba says the mind is an instrument, and the five bodily senses of sight, hearing, taste, smell, and touch are also instruments, and they should all be used together to gather information about the external world. Of these, the mind is the master instrument that should control and direct the senses. But instead, it usually serves the senses, even though they should rightfully be its servants. It is this reversal of roles that leads us into bondage. To quote Baba again, "The characteristic of the mind is to flutter and flit hither and thither through the outlets of the senses into the external world of color, sound, taste, smell, and touch. It tends to allow the senses to lead it into attachment to outer objects, and thus desire for those objects is born. But all desires originate in the bodily or physical form in which the real Self merely resides. However, the mind can be tamed and turned toward the High Self as its master and guide."

Another way in which Baba describes the mind is, "Mind is not like a white paper that does not have any impressions written on it. The tendencies and experiences derived in a number of births have been imprinted on it. The fruits of many actions performed by the body are also imprinted on the mind. Therefore, mind may be described as an entity that is full of thoughts and desires." So the mind is not the real Self any more than is the body. They are both instruments designed for the use of the High Self.

The senses can be likened to a team of horses pulling a vehicle, with the mind as the driver. When the horses are allowed free rein, they are likely to run off in different directions to pursue a tempting scent, follow a distracting sound, or gallop back to the stable to be fed. If we actually found ourselves in such a vehicle, we would not feel at all safe or secure. Yet many people spend their lives allowing their senses to lead them astray. The horses need a driver giving orders to ensure that they act in unison, as a team proceeding in the same direction, so the vehicle can safely reach its intended destination. By far the most reliable way to achieve this objective is for the driver to hold the reins lightly and give over the actual driving to the High Self, who is so much more capable of handling the entire process.

Baba sums up the role of the mind succinctly when he says, "The mind is said to be the instrument of both bondage and liberation. Allow the senses to lead it outward; it binds. Allow the intelligence to prevail upon it to look inward for bliss; it liberates."

Another of Baba's graphic word pictures is in the form of a warning: "When air fills a football, it takes the form of the ball. When it fills a balloon, it takes the form of the balloon—oval, sausage-shaped, or spherical. The mind assumes the form of the objects to which it is attached. If it gets fixed on small things, it becomes small; if on grand things, it becomes grand. Like the camera, it takes a picture of whatever it is pointed at, so take care before you click."

Beloved Baba take my hand
As I hold it up to you.
Dispel the cloud of Maya
Which obscures you from my view.

My inner Self and you are one,
Which in my heart I know.
I also know to reach that state
I must be pure as snow.

But on my own I cannot weld
My human will to thine,
So this is why I seek your help
To detach it from all mine.

Help me dear Baba to let go
Of my imaginary needs
And I will try to turn from all
On which my ego feeds.

And as I reach up high to you,
Please take my hand in yours
Until I'm empty of myself
And my lightened spirit soars.

But when I first catch sight of that
Which seers call the light,
I may be overwhelmed by it
So hold me very tight.

In pouring out my heart to you
I've lost that cloud so dark
So I'll now relax in quiet relief
Till my soul soars like a lark.

Chapter 3

The Organ-Grinder's Monkey

Not long after I started to write this book, my husband and I went away for the weekend to northern California. We planned to have lunch at a nearby wharf, so Sidney dropped me off to wait for him while he parked the car. To my complete astonishment, right in front of where I stood was an organ-grinder with his little performing monkey. I could hardly believe my eyes, for I cannot recall having seen one since I left England, or maybe even since I was a child.

I was fascinated as the man ground out the tune on his hand organ while his little companion—clad in a tiny suit, complete with hat and harness—with the leash held in its master's hand, performed for the audience. Several parents and their children had gathered to watch as the monkey did its tricks, concluding the show by shaking the hand of each child at its master's bidding. I guessed that many of the children were seeing such a sight for the first time and were delighted. But to me, it seemed like an excellent example of how our monkey minds must be harnessed and brought under control instead of being allowed to run wild and get into all kinds of mischief, as both monkeys and minds are apt to do.

While working in my usual way with a male client just a few days after this incident, I asked, as usual, to be shown whatever would be of help to him at that particular time. An enormous figure of Hanuman appeared on my inner scene, apparently to preside over the session. In a prior meeting with the same man, I had been shown a clear, deep, green pool for him to use to still his mind. He was to concentrate on the smooth surface of the water and watch the occasional ripple arise and eventually dissipate. As soon as Hanuman appeared, I was led back to the pool and became aware of this same man sitting beside it, leaning over to look into its depths. But to my surprise, as I caught sight of his reflection in the water, I saw that he had a small monkey squatting on his left shoulder, whispering into his ear.

When I related this picture to him, he immediately agreed that he did indeed have "a monkey on his back," as he expressed it. He went on to tell me that he had even caught a glimpse of it out of the corner of his eye that very morning and had mentioned it to his wife. As he proceeded to connect it to an addictive behavior pattern that had persisted despite every effort on his part to break it, the memory of the organ-grinder and his pet monkey flashed back into my mind. It seemed to present the perfect solution to his dilemma. So I suggeseted that with the aid of "active imagination" he could dress the monkey he had perceived, put a harness on it, hold the leash to control its movement. He could then begin to teach it to take its cue from the example of Hanuman by devoting its time and energy to serving whatever symbol he had chosen to depict the High Self.

However, the scene is not only true for this man, but is also valid for the majority of people who are led astray by their monkey minds. They need to take responsibility for reining in the monkey's tendency to roam compulsively, tempting them to become attached—and possibly addicted—to whatever they see that excites their desire to possess it by grabbing it and not letting go.

A little later in the same session, I remembered the three little carved wooden monkeys that used to sit on the mantlepiece in the living room of the house where I grew up in England. One monkey held its hands over its eyes, one covered its ears with its hands, and the third placed both hands over its mouth. The theme was, "See no evil;

hear no evil; speak no evil." I had seen them every day for many years, yet had never really understood their message and certainly had not applied it. But now, as the memory of them came back into my mind, I realized that they, too, represent the need to control the three senses of seeing, hearing, and tasting—with the additional aspect of speaking—lest they lead the mind to attach itself to the objects they reveal to it.

Chapter 4

Hanuman

In the *Ramayana*, one of the ancient Hindu epics, Hanuman is introduced as the Monkey God, son of the Wind God. He is famous for his complete and undeviating devotion to Rama, who represents God immanent in all living beings. Baba describes Hanuman as the embodiment of courage. His importance to human beings is his inspiring example of how our monkey minds can be brought under control by unswerving service to our Higher Self.

As a monkey, he represents our instinctive or animal nature, with all its cravings and attachments. But, by his example, he shows the way out of that dilemma. By dedicating his entire life to serving Rama, he succeeded in harnessing his animal nature to the Atma, or God-within, and by so doing he was able to raise his consciousness from the instinctual, unconscious level up to that of the conscious and evolved human being. He leads the way so that we too, if we so desire, may follow his example and escape from the trap in which we have allowed ourselves to be caught by our own greed and attachment to the material world.

The following whimsical little story about Hanuman, taken from Baba's version of the Ramayana, clearly illustrates this point: "After the coronation, one day, Sita and the three brothers of Rama met and planned to exclude Hanuman from the *seva* (service) of Rama. They wanted all the various services from Rama to be divided only among themselves. They felt that Hanuman had enough chances already. So, they drew up a list—as exhaustive as they could remember—of the services from dawn till dusk, down to the smallest minutiae and assigned each item to one among themselves. They presented the list of items and assignees to the Lord while Hanuman was present. Rama heard about the new procedure, read the list, and gave his approval with a smile. He told Hanuman that all the tasks had been assigned to others and that he could now take a rest. Hanuman prayed that the list might be read, and when it was done he noticed an omission—the task of 'snapping the fingers when one yawns.' Of course, being an emperor, Rama should not be allowed to do it for himself. 'It has to be done by a servant,' he pleaded. Rama agreed to allot the task to Hanuman.

"It was a great piece of luck for Hanuman, for it entailed his constant attendance on his master, for how could anyone predict when the yawn would come? And he had to be looking on that heart-charming face all the time to be ready with the snap, as soon as the yawn was on. He could not run away for a minute, nor could he relax for a moment. You must be happy that the *seva* of the Lord keeps you always in His presence and ever vigilant to carry out His behests!"

Another of Baba's short stories, titled "Whoever Surrenders, Rama Accepts," illustrates this same point. "God is so merciful that He will come ten steps toward you if you but take one step toward Him. Vibhishana, the brother of Ravana, inquired from Hanuman whether Rama will accept his homage and take him under His protecting shade. He said, 'I am the brother of His worst enemy, whom He has vowed to destroy. I am a member of the demonic race. I am unacquainted with the Vedas or Sastras, or the rituals of the Aryas.' Then Hanuman replied, 'Oh you fool! Do you think He cares for ritual rectitude, or family status, or scholarship? If so, how could He accept me, a monkey?' " There are many other stories about Hanuman, all illustrating the same facet of the ancient teaching that we should defer to Rama or our true Self.

In my work, when in a reverie state I have been introduced to many enlightened beings in their personified forms. Some of them are recognizable from the ancient writings of different cultures, while others are not familiar to me. When I first became aware of them gathered together in a vast assembly, I was astonished that their size varied so remarkably. Some appeared to be towering figures thirty or more feet in height. Others, though still imposingly tall, seemed to be around ten or twelve feet high, while still others were considerably shorter, though nonetheless impressive. At the time, I wondered about the great differences in height but did not question it, as I have learned when working in this way to keep my conscious mind, with all its questions and doubts, quiescent. Only then can I concentrate on whatever I am being taught with the least possible interference. In that way, whatever I need to know will be shown to me when the time is right for it to be revealed. This aspect of the work I can genuinely trust.

Shortly after my first introduction to these heavenly helpers, wise ones, or specialists, I was talking on the telephone to a Sai devotee. Out of a clear blue sky, he shared an interesting observation with me that he had heard Baba make in a talk to the boys attending one of his colleges. He was relating some of the old stories from the Indian epics. At one point he interrupted the flow of the story he was telling to observe that at the time of the Avatar Rama the people were over thirty feet tall, while at the time of Krishna the people were around twelve feet tall, and since those times human beings have gradually become shorter.

When I heard this, I literally gasped, as it concurred exactly with the view of them I had been given in the reveries. It so happens that the figure of Hanuman had become a frequent visitor to supply his particular energy and help whenever needed. He was one of those who were thirty feet or more in height and a most impressive sight to behold. It was quite a relief to have the height corroborated in this unexpected way by Baba through my friend.

When I was present a few days before Baba's 65th birthday at the dedication of the huge statue of Hanuman, I was entranced at the sight of him towering up into the sky. I bent back my head to look up at him far above me and was again grateful to have my reverie view of him substantiated in this dramatic way. However, the fleeting thought crossed my mind that one thing about this statue was not exactly as I had observed in my reveries. His head did not seem to be quite large enough to conform to the rest of his magnificent form. But, came the quick thought, who am I to criticize? Obviously, Baba had ordered it to be made and must surely have given precise instructions for the correct proportions. I felt guilty even to be questioning it and quickly suppressed the doubt. Imagine my utter amazement when a friend who was also present at the inaugural ceremony casually mentioned to me on the following day that as Baba passed by after the ceremony he had commented that the head was too small. I could hardly believe my ears. Here again, I was reassured that I had not imagined it. What a gift!

Then, soon after we returned home I was talking to another friend, an artist who also goes to India from time to time to see Baba. He told me that the last time he was there he had painted a picture of Hanuman embracing Rama and had given it to Baba. He scrutinized it very carefully and pronounced it to be a very good painting, then, after a pause, he added almost apologetically, "But Hanuman had monkey's hands, not human ones," as the artist had portrayed them.

So, we have Hanuman as a guide to lead us to defer to the High Self or Rama and to help us detach ourselves from the lure of everything that our monkey minds grasp and refuse to release. Hanuman is an excellent model of one whose life was dedicated to serving Rama. He was absolutely devoted, always willing and, indeed, eager to serve him in any way possible, and placed Rama's wishes above those of anyone else, including his own. So great was his devotion that he was constantly on the watch for any opportunity to serve his beloved master. In this way he sets an inspiring example for all of us and shows us our true goal in life: devotion to the High Self, which Rama represents.

However, as Baba repeatedly reminds us, we are all God or Rama in actuality. He urges us to spend our lives in service to others, though this does not refer to personalities, but to the God within the outer covering seen as the human being. This kind of service, he avers, is real worship of God. He has given us two main programs designed to help us identify with our High Self more and more of the time, until it becomes a continuous habit and we eventually merge with It. The two suggested programs are Ceiling on Desires and Selfless Service, each of which will be considered in more detail in later chapters.

Chapter 5

The Senses

Baba says, "The senses are the prime motive forces for the mind and the illusion it suffers from." The senses connect us to exterior objects as well as people, places, food, entertainment, plans, and a myriad of other distractions. The list is endless and different for each individual. Once connected, we yearn to own whatever we have become attached to. But, invariably, when we do possess the object of our desire, the attachment often becomes so strong that it ends up owning us instead of the reverse. Carried to the extreme this situation leads to addictions.

Baba also tells us we have "spun a web around our true essence with our thoughts tied to our desires. Many are mummified when the layer upon layer becomes crystallized, which makes it harder to chip away." We share the senses with all living creatures. They are valuable instruments that enable us to make contact with and evaluate our surroundings. They act as important indicators to alert us to danger to our physical body. They are, therefore, designed to assure our survival in the particular environment in which we find ourselves, and to help us adjust and avoid the various dangers inherent therein. They are attentive servants as long as we retain the role of the master and control their activities.

Most animals possess acute eyesight, which enables them to see if a predator is approaching by the movement of grass or bushes, or the shape or color of its body against the surrounding terrain. The same applies to the senses of hearing and smell, both of which alert an animal to danger. Its ears may pick up the sound of twigs snapping or dry leaves crackling under the weight of an approaching animal foraging for food. When the wind is blowing in the right direction, the scent of a possible enemy will be noted by the sense of smell, allowing time enough to escape. The sense of smell also proves useful in determining whether certain foods are safe to eat or should be avoided. Animals always smell food before they will attempt to eat it, and if its odor has diminished they will leave it untouched. The sense of taste is also an accurate indicator of whether food is good to eat. The sense of touch warns creatures of changes in temperature, sharp thorns, and other hazards.

When accepted as helpful servants, the senses are valuable assets. It is when we follow them blindly and are led to become attached to whatever they are attached to that problems arise. So, when considering how to regain control over them, we need to ascertain where they have led us and therefore what we deem indispensable to our sense of well-being. What would we find the hardest thing to be without? The answer to this question will be different for individuals according to particular likes and dislikes. "One man's meat is another man's poison" expresses this truth very clearly. Consequently, we should observe for ourselves how we react to what the five senses bring to our attention, either with attraction or revulsion.

However, this is not to imply that we should deprive ourselves of those essential objects that serve a useful purpose or give us pleasure. It is more a matter of carefully watching to ensure that we do not become so attached to certain things that they control us and our behavior, like the monkey with its fist caught in the bottle. We should retain control and avoid surrendering it to anyone or anything, for to do so means we are enslaved by whatever we are attached to. It is also essential to use discrimination to determine which things are useful or appropriate in our lives and which ones are superfluous or deleterious to our well-being.

It is obvious that most of the problems we face stem from unrequited or thwarted desires, which creates a perfect breeding ground for such negative emotions as greed, envy, jealousy, anger, and all the rest. So we definitely need to find a way to put a stop to this chain reaction that shackles us just as effectively as if we were bound hand and foot and locked in a cell—a prison of our own making.

Chapter 6

Baba's Ceiling on Desires Program

Baba has presented us with a very clear and simple outline to help us to start to detach ourselves from our monkey minds. He does not expect us to give up immediately all our desires and attachments, for he is well aware that it would be too drastic a step. So, he has suggested we use a program called "Ceiling on Desires" to help us begin in a small way to trim down our desires, and in so doing to start letting go of what he calls "our excess luggage." He says, "Desires are like luggage. 'Less luggage more comfort, makes travel a pleasure,' as the railway reminds you. If you have to lessen luggage for a short railway journey, how much more urgent it is to lessen the luggage when you are on the much longer journey of life."

He repeatedly refers to the four main areas of our lives that are constantly being controlled by our desires; namely, the way we handle money, food, time, and energy. He points out that in the lives of many people, except the very poor, there is a shocking amount of waste that should be reduced to a minimum in these four areas. He acknowledges that everyone needs a certain amount of money and food to survive, but that few individuals are sufficiently disciplined to accept limits or budgets. *Budget* has become an unwelcome word to many people and implies rigorous self-denial. This attitude is often the result of having had budgets too strictly imposed during childhood without clear and understandable reasons being supplied.

The Ceiling on Desires program is designed to help each individual, and hence each family, live happier and more fulfilling lives. Instead of wasting life and its gifts, it can enable those who are willing to follow it to have more money, more food, more time, and more energy at their disposal, thus making their lives less stressful and consequently healthier and happier. We need to become aware of whether any or all of these four gifts are being wasted in nonessential or unhealthy ways, and begin to use them more wisely for the benefit of ourselves and the members of our family. An added bonus will be the gradual detachment from the ego- and body-inspired desires that keep our monkey minds so active.

Baba has often said, "I will give you what you want, hoping you will want what I have come to give you." We may say we want enlightenment, but in order to achieve that state we need to give up our attachment to our ego and its desires.

Baba also says, "The main reason some people turn away from me is not because they have lost their love for me. It is because their wishes have not been fulfilled. They are gripped with fear that if they are with me, their worldly wishes and desires may not be fulfilled. So they go away." But this fear, like most other fears, is not founded in truth. It is we ourselves who often put a limit on what Baba will give us, either by insisting that we must have certain things or by refusing to accept others. But what we do not understand is that in many instances, what we think we want does not always turn out to be beneficial or even pleasing. Likewise, what we think we do not want may surprise us by proving to be helpful and even rewarding. Our personal view of what we need or do not need is very shortsighted. When we insist on pursuing any object of our desire, or endeavor to avoid whatever we consider unwelcome, we are very possibly preventing those very experiences we most need for our learning from coming our way to teach us.

Since Baba represents, in human form, the indwelling God that is our true identity, it is much easier and certainly much safer to surrender to his better judgment of what we need, and to stop insisting on whatever our egos want. For, from past experience, our choices have usually proved to be disappointing in the long run, despite how alluring they promised to be when we first entertained them.

Please give me what you know I need
Though I may not yet agree
From my restricted vision
That it is best for me.

We tend to hold too tightly
To those things we think we need,
And forget that you know better
Since our past lives you can read.

We also try to push away
Those things we label sad,
Not seeing that they also hold
Some good beneath the bad.

You tell us to be willing
To observe each one and see
That it's better to accept them both
With equanimity.

For only if we do so
Can we ever really be
Completely happy and secure
In your uncertainty.

So give me what you know I need
And help me to agree
That only you are able
To decide what's best for me.

Chapter 7

The Black and White Birds

I was once given a wonderfully clear insight to illustrate how we so often lose our equanimity when we reach out to grab with our monkey minds those things we think we cannot live without and push away from us whatever it is we most fear. I call it, "The Black and White Birds."

On my inner scene, it appeared to me that I was walking along a tightrope with my arms stretched out to either side to help me retain my balance. I was carefully placing one foot after the other on the rope, making certain to keep my gaze directly ahead without looking down. Suddenly, out of the corner of my eye, I glimpsed a huge black bird that looked as if it were about to attack me from my left side. Without any hesitation, I leaned over toward it to push it away and promptly fell off the tightrope. I had climbed back on and continued to walk across it, when I caught sight of a beautiful, gleaming, pure white bird on my right side. It was so appealing that I wanted to touch it and impulsively leaned over to take hold of it, only to fall off the tightrope again.

Again, I climbed back and asked for the meaning of this inner experience to be revealed to me. I received the intimation that the black bird represented everything I did not want or most feared might happen, whereas the white bird symbolized everything I could ever wish for. By either repulsing the black bird or grasping the white bird, I lost my balance. When I asked to be given a solution to this common dilemma, I was directed to get back up onto the tightrope and, with my arms outstretched to either side—

with the palms held up and open—to be willing to accept whichever of the two birds wished to settle on them.

This experience dramatically illustrates Baba's repeated advice to accept all the pairs of opposites, such as heat and cold, pleasure and pain, health and sickness, and all the rest with equanimity. One of his little catchphrases sums up this point so well: "Praise and blame; all the same." However, it is easier to hear this advice, or read about it, than to put it into practice in our lives. Only with Baba's help is that possible, for the ego will fight giving up its control to the very end. A little mantra that has come through the work in which I am involved—"Surrender, Trust, and Accept"—is a great help. It means surrender to the High Self, trust It to bring about whatever It knows is needed, and accept whatever that may be.

Surrender and trust. Surrender and trust.
We know that we should, but we rarely do.
To try to accomplish it we must
For we know that Baba wants us to.

What is it in us that gets in the way
Of total surrender to his will?
Desires and ego Baba will say,
Which we must discover how to kill.

But how can we manage this difficult task
Of letting go of our fondest dreams?
Baba will help us if we ask,
But we must be willing to give him the means.

We cling to people and places and things
As sources of our security.
He gives us vibhuti, medallions, and rings
To link us to him for eternity.

With surrender and trust from morning to night
Our lives will take on a brand new lease
And we'll discover, to our delight
That we have exchanged our worries for peace.

Chapter 8

Selfless Service—
An Antidote for the Monkey Mind

In addition to the reduction of waste through the Ceiling on Desires program, Baba suggests that we use the savings thus made possible in all four categories to help those who are less fortunate than ourselves. It is certainly not difficult to find people who need help, particularly in this day and age. In this way, two of Baba's pet projects can be combined: "Ceiling on Desires" and "Selfless Seva." Baba specifies that it should be literally selfless service rather than giving out of self-interest, which contaminates it and causes it to recoil on the one who serves instead of furthering progress toward enlightenment.

Many people say they would like to be more useful in the world by helping the starving, homeless, unhappy, sick, or abused. But that is often where their good intentions end. Numerous excuses are forthcoming to absolve them from guilt or other people's criticism. For example, they cannot afford to help because they are raising a family, and every penny is already accounted for in a tight budget. Or, they are far too busy and too tired from working so hard to provide the necessities for themselves and their families and lack the extra time and energy to do anything more than their daily routine demands of them. This is indeed a common situation at the present time throughout the world. However, when the Ceiling on Desires program is followed, most people discover to their amazement that they not only have extra money, but are better nourished, have more time, and best of all, by saving energy they are not too tired to share their savings with those who are in distress. In addition, when people start to engage in some kind of service to humanity, they invariably report that they themselves are the ones who benefit most from such involvement, and to a far greater extent than the recipients of their service. Sharing whatever we have with others— whether it is money, food, time, energy, or knowledge and insight—produces unimagined dividends.

A further unexpected bonus accrues from such selfless service. When we are busily engaged in giving to others, we are completely reversing the direction of the monkey mind. By concentrating on alleviating the distress of others instead of craving and grabbing whatever we desire, the monkey mind, like Hanuman, is turned toward the God-self within. For by serving others we are actually serving the God within all beings, since at that level all are one.

When asked his identity, Hanuman's immediate reply was always, "I am the servant of Rama." So by engaging in selfless service, we too can begin to turn to the occupant within our desire-filled bodies and serve the Rama, Christ, Baba, Buddha, or any other name by which we identify the God-Self resident in both ourselves and in all whom we attempt to help, whether human or animal.

But, the old saying, "Charity begins at home," is a good motto to adopt. It is a common occurrence for some-one to be a ministering angel to so-called strangers, earn-ing their undying gratitude and approval, while the members of the family are neglected, their needs unmet, and their requests for help either ignored or responded to with impatience, anger, or irritation from the "popular angel." But, Baba tells us that the individuals with whom we spend the major part of our lives are the very ones who can teach us exactly what we need to learn, if only we will recognize this fact and allow the learning to take place. So, those who are closely associated with us can very well be our greatest teachers. If, with their help, we can learn patience, tolerance, steadfastness, and forbearance in our family relationships, our lives will be as helpful in providing us with the spiritual education we most need as would a life as a sadhu or renunciate.

Service, whether to family members or others, should be undertaken for the right reasons and not with any ulterior motive in mind, for that would curtail its effectiveness. To be free from ego it should flow out of deep compassion for the pain, hunger, feelings of rejection, loss, or any other problem from which either an individual or a group is suffering. Only then will it benefit the one who serves as well as those receiving the services. Therefore, care needs to be taken against deciding to engage in a particular service in order to feel important or worthwhile, to gain recognition, gratitude, or any other reward from the beneficiaries, or for spiritual or personal gain of any kind. It should be free from selfish motives such as providing an escape from boredom or from the daily routine and its responsibilities.

Another most important point that needs to be remembered is the necessity to remain detached from the results of our service, whether successful or otherwise. Baba tells us, "Do not become inflated with success or punctured by failure."

The very best antidote for the monkey mind is to follow the example set by Hanuman, which is to be the servant of the real Self, by whatever name we choose to refer to It. Baba urges us to "take Hanuman as your example of service, for he stands out as a supreme example of dedicated service to the Divine. He was strong, learned, and virtuous but had no trace of pride." Baba also tells us that service is the only method for combating the effects of the *Kali Yuga* (the darkest of the four yugas, or ages in which we are living), and that all other methods designed to further our spiritual progress are inferior to selfless service. He further explains that "spiritual exercises like repeating God's name, meditation, *yagna*, reading the scriptures, or undertaking pilgrimages are not equal to the performance of selfless service," and "activity in the shape of service charged with love fulfills the aims of all paths to the Godhead. It is a more exalted means of spiritual progress than such other ways as meditation, *bhajan*, and yoga."

So, wherever we become aware of a need or a chance to help we should waste no time in accepting it, bearing in mind that, like Hanuman, we are serving the God within whomever we serve, and we are also serving the God within ourselves.

We habitually think of me and mine
Instead of we and ours.
We labor under the false belief
That our egos contain our powers.

But if only we can remember
To turn from me to you
We can break our lifelong habit,
And let the inner light shine through.

Chapter 9

Waste of Money

In his Ceiling on Desires program, Baba listed money first, presumably because the amount we have at our disposal determines, to a large extent, how we manage the other three categories of food, time, and energy. He observes that in this one respect, the poor are more fortunate than the wealthy. Since they have less money, they also have fewer temptations or opportunities to be wasteful. For instance, in third world countries there is neither the pressure nor the enticements to which more affluent societies are exposed.

With many people on a spiritual path, there seems to be a misunderstanding concerning the place of money in their lives. Money in itself is neither positive nor negative. It is neutral, so its effect depends on how it is used. If it allows us to work out our particular destiny and learn how to become free from attachment to it as a security symbol, it can have a positive effect. If, on the other hand, we allow it to control us and our behavior to such an extent that we are led to selfishness or wrongdoing, then it can have a negative influence on us. But the decision is ours alone, and we cannot blame or praise the money. Yes, it can be the root of all evil and frequently is. But, the reverse is also true, for if it is used wisely and appropriately, it can greatly enhance life by freeing us to concentrate on living like Hanuman, devoted to the will of the High Self or Rama.

Because we are surrounded by an excess of material objects, we are constantly bombarded, through the media, to buy things we hope will immediately satisfy our earthly desires and make us happy forevermore. But our desires stem from our mistaken identification with our bodies and the five senses tempting us all day long.

Baba says, "In the day-to-day life, everyone requires money. But it is something like wearing a shoe. The shoe must be of the correct size. If it is too loose, you will not be able to walk comfortably. If it is too tight, you will also feel uncomfortable. It is a problem if you have excessive money. If you have a shortage, that also is a difficult situation. Man often becomes a slave to money while trying to earn more than he needs." And he further states, "When you are adding to your bank account further and further sums of money, you are making it harder for your children to lead clean, comfortable, and honorable lives." He also says, "Money has to be given its own place of importance. It has to be used in the best way possible. Because if you do not make the best of any given thing, you cannot understand what it is there for. You should, for instance, use the power of intelligence to avoid the misuse of money."

When we allow ourselves to become attached to money we will find it to be unreliable, like all other illusory security symbols. We can also be so attached to what money can buy that we are lured into equating our worth with how much money or how many possessions we have. We forget who we really are: the indestructible Self.

When considering how to stop wasting money, we first need to discover how we are spending it, for one of the main obstacles to budgeting is the lack of any definite idea of how our money is being spent. So, the very first step is to compile a list of current expenditures to reveal a clearer picture of the main ones. This list should start with the regular, basic, ongoing expenses such as rent or mortgage payments, insurance, taxes, utilities, telephone, food, clothing, education, medical services, and so forth. Each individual's list will vary according to the person compiling it. Age, job, responsibilities, marital status, number of children, position in society, family background, and many other factors will all have their respective influence.

Once weekly, monthly, and yearly outlays have been determined the remainder of the income is revealed. This is the area where waste is most likely to occur and where our desires can lead us astray if they are immediately gratified without due consideration of the consequences. After the list of expenditures has been initiated, a pattern will begin to emerge that will clarify the areas where waste is taking place.

Since our five senses are responsible for enticing the mind to become attached to whatever they themselves are attracted to, it is important to recognize the role of the senses when embarking on the Ceiling on Desires program. For, as Baba expresses it, "When the senses, which should be man's servants, have instead become the masters, he has become the slave to external beauty, evanescent melody, exterior softness, tickling taste, and fragile fragrance." So, when considering waste of money we need to discover how all five senses tempt the monkey mind to become attached to the multitude of sights, sounds, smells, tastes, and tactile sensations they present to it.

The Sense of Sight and Waste of Money

Sight is, for most people, their most strongly developed sense and is therefore the one that leads to the most attachments, which in turn leads to waste. Advertising—a campaign of persuasion—is one of the chief ways by which the eyes lead the mind to become attached to whatever is attractive to each individual from among the host of possibilities presented to us. In newspapers and magazines, catalogues and fliers sent through the mail, billboards along the highways, and, even more convincingly, in television commercials, manufacturers advertise their wares by having them displayed so attractively that viewers are persuaded to hurry to a store to buy them, whether they really need them or not.

Since these commercials contribute most of the financial support to programs devoted to entertainment and other topics, they wield a great deal of power and have full control over advertising techniques. There is, therefore, an additional coercion at work besides the attraction of the items on display. It is control by the manufacturers over the unseen people in the audience, whom they are urging to spend money on their merchandise, often wastefully. It may be attractive clothes that are being shown, beautiful jewelry, the latest models of shiny new cars, delicious-looking food, cosmetics guaranteed to delay the aging process, electronics, or a host of other alluring items. The list is unending and varied, designed as it is to tempt all types of people.

Even children are not spared this merciless barrage. They have become the latest target of advertisers who plan how best to tempt them with all sorts of products and merchandise. The children then beg, cajole, and in some cases even bully their parents into buying them the articles displayed on the screen, even though these may not be things they really need or even want. They are being pressured to possess them because they think their friends, who are also being bombarded by the same commercials, will try to persuade their parents to buy them. Children generally do not want to be different from their peers, feel rejected by them, or be underprivileged; facts of which the advertisers are acutely aware. In this way, children are being programmed from a very early age to believe they should have whatever they see. This habit of instant gratification often persists into adulthood, when it is much more difficult to erase.

But advertising, though a very potent persuader, is not the only way the eyes lead the mind to crave whatever they see. Department stores and supermarkets, and to a lesser extent smaller stores, are another source of temptation to waste money through the sense of sight. The eyes are dazzled by the huge displays of merchandise set out so artfully to attract attention. The array is bewildering, for it presents so many choices to further confuse the shopper on whom it acts in an almost hypnotic way. The host of items is placed on display with the sole purpose of luring people to buy them, whether they need or even like them. It takes a very strong person to resist such potent coercion.

Sales are even more of a hazard for those who are addicted to shopping, for they offer the added attraction of obtaining bargains. Sadly, many people succumb to this alluring decoy, believing they will save the amount of money by which the item is reduced, overlooking the fact that unless they can use it, instead of saving money they have actually wasted it.

In addition, we are literally surrounded with sights—both pleasant and unpleasant—every time we walk in the streets, drive our cars along the highways, go to the market or other stores, work at jobs, visit friends, travel further afield, and engage in all the activities that comprise our daily routine. In all of these situations, we may see many kinds of things that are pleasing to behold and therefore tempting us to own them.

The Sense of Hearing and Waste of Money

How does the sense of hearing tempt us to waste money? As with the sense of sight, television is one of the major ways advertisers persuade listeners to buy their products. These items are extolled in the commercials. In a sales pitch the announcer may be describing a new time-saving appliance, the very latest computer model, a trip to some exotic far-off paradise promising temporary escape from the stress of daily life, or any of a multitude of other attractions that are touted over the air.

In addition, the radio turned on in the car while driving to work, attending to errands, taking the children to school or to after-school activities, and all the other daily trips, provides advertisers with yet another seductive method of urging both the driver and passengers to buy whatever is being glowingly described by the announcer in a most persuasive tone of voice.

Even private telephone lines are now being used by advertisers. Salespeople do their utmost to prevail upon consumers to purchase aluminum siding or magazine subscriptions, buy shares in a certain company, send for an exciting new product, or invest in some other venture or item. With this method of advertising, there is the additional advantage of personal contact, which has been used for centuries to hypnotize likely subjects to follow vocal commands; in this instance, those of a speaker who has been well trained in the art of persuasion. Interestingly enough, these calls are invariably placed around the time of the evening meal, when it is assumed that an adult member of the family is most likely to be at home.

Then there is simple word-of-mouth advertising, which occurs when people regale whoever will listen with descriptive lists of their latest acquisitions. Infected by this enthusiasm, their listeners may be envious, jealous, or competitive, and desire for themselves what they hear being described. Or, someone may tell of a new venture that promises to provide a sizable monetary return, and those who hear about it are attracted by the prospect of having more money to spend, and decide to invest in it themselves.

These are just a few of the ways the sense of hearing can lure people to waste money unless they use discrimination to decide for themselves if they really need the proffered products.

The Sense of Smell and Waste of Money

According to my dictionary "the sense of smell enables a substance to be perceived through the chemical stimulation of the olfactory nerves in the nasal cavity, by particles given off by the substance in question." Not only does our sense of smell protect us from harm by noxious substances, it frequently tempts us to acquire those things that smell sweet, such as costly perfumes, certain foods, tobacco, coffee, and many other attractively smelling items.

Advertisers are quick to take advantage of their potential customer's sense of smell. Foods, such as breads and other bakery products may contain chemicals that enhance their olfactory appeal and encourage people to choose one particular brand over those that smell less appealing. We are all aware of the samples of perfumes included in catalogues, and even in bills from department stores, to lure recipients to buy a particular brand. Recently this practice has been heavily criticized for causing unpleasant reactions in those people who happen to be allergic to the ingredients in many perfumes.

Only if customers fall prey to this campaign and allow their sense of smell to lead them to be extravagant, buy too much or too many, purchase items they cannot use or those currently in fashion simply to impress their acquaintances does it lead to a waste of money. Again, discrimination is essential to keep purchases within acceptable limits and to retain control of one's sense of smell.

The Sense of Taste and Waste of Money

Taste and smell are closely connected. Those people who have lost their sense of smell report that they no longer have as strong an ability to taste their food and often become uninterested in eating. This is due to the fact that the smell of food stimulates the secretions from salivary glands, which aid in the digestive process that starts in the mouth. Most people have experienced the whetting of their appetite when they smell the mouth-watering aroma of baking bread, onions being fried, or coffee brewing.

But in addition to taste being associated with items of food and drink, it has also become a common practice to use the word *taste* in other connections. We may have a taste for something, meaning we find it pleasurable, such as a certain type of entertainment, a sport, or some other activity that appeals to us. We may be described as having good taste in our choice of clothing, furniture, jewelry, or literature. Or, we may remark that we want something so badly we can almost taste it.

It is therefore necessary to determine how this multifaceted sense of taste leads the mind toward pursuits that waste money. This does not mean, however, that we should not enjoy the taste of food—since enjoyment aids digestion by stimulating the necessary secretions—nor need we feel we should not enjoy other pleasurable pursuits. It is only when we allow the sense of taste to control us and cause craving for certain items to excess that we become guilty of wasting money by buying more than we need, more than we use, or more than we can afford.

The Sense of Touch and Waste of Money

The sense of touch relates to the skin, and is stimulated by anything that causes a feeling of pleasure or pain in any part of the body. The skin covers the entire body, so reactions to heat and cold, dryness and dampness, and all the variations of climatic conditions stimulate the sense of touch. People have different likes and dislikes. This fact also applies to the various textures of clothing or other materials that come in contact with the skin on different parts of the body. Such textures as smooth, soft, rough, prickly, and all the others cause a wide variety of reactions in different people.

The sense of touch is stimulated from birth by parents holding, caressing, stroking and massaging, and touching the baby. Both unpleasant and pleasurable touching will lay down patterns that will continue into adulthood. If a baby has been pleasantly satisfied in infancy and given the security of being loved, it will not be as likely to crave being touched as an adult or to avoid such contact.

As with the other senses, only when the sense of touch leads the mind to become unduly attached to a sensation does it entice us to waste money by buying something appealing to the touch, even though we cannot afford it or derive sufficient benefit to warrant its cost. Again, if something controls the mind so that our thoughts are always straying to it—and it becomes responsible for our addiction to a reaction to touch—then it renders us its slave and can lead directly to a waste of money in satisfying the craving thus developed.

You turn away your faces
To look upon the earth
And I am left without your love
Which is your only worth.

You give your love to humans
And expect theirs in return.
My love you have already
But it you often spurn.

When will you ever waken
And turn to look my way
And accept the love I offer you
On each and every day?

My love alone can satisfy
Your deepest human need
And in return I seek from you
Your love on which I feed.

Chapter 10

Waste of Food

It is easy to see that the amount of money available at any given time influences many other areas of life, not the least being the quantity and quality of food and drink available. However, except in extreme cases, it does not necessarily pose an impossible problem if wise planning and a firm determination to cut out waste is initiated.

But food, in the broadest sense, means anything taken into a person from outside. As Baba expresses it, "The calories that one takes in through the mouth are but a small part of the intake of man. The intake by the senses are part of the food that builds the individual. The sounds heard, the sights seen, the tactile impressions sought or suffered, the air breathed, the environment that presses for attention, appreciation, and adoption—all these are food. They have considerable impact on the character and career of the individual. Eat to live and do not believe that you live in order to eat."

In other words, all that we ingest with our five senses— music and words we hear with our ears, movies and books we see and read with our eyes, odors we smell, food and drink we taste, and materials and things we touch—need to be considered when attempting to eliminate waste from our lives to determine whether they are necessary, or even desirable. The food we eat and the liquids we drink provide the fuel that keeps the body in good health and functioning effectively, if they are not indulged in to excess.

According to Baba, "All the variety in taste, color, and smell of the multiform items of food is, when you consider it fairly and squarely, a mere drug to cure the illness of hunger. All the drinks that man has invented are but drugs to alleviate the illness of thirst. Man suffers from the fever of the senses and tries the quick remedies of recreations, pleasures, picnics, banquets, dances, etc., only to find that the fever does not subside."

Baba has also summed up, in his usual clear and simple way, the effect of excesses related to food or drink; in this instance, drink. "When man puts the contents of the bottle in man, he himself gets into the bottle and cannot escape! First, man drinks wine, then the wine drinks more wine, and finally the wine drinks man himself. He is sunk and drowned in drink."

It is becoming more and more evident that increasing numbers of people all over the world are suffering from malnutrition. This is true even in the more affluent countries, due to the fact that much of the food available is highly processed and lacking assimilable nourishment. The modern junk-food or fast-food phenomenon is prevalent everywhere. It is often a direct result of the fast pace of living that leaves many people with too little time to plan, purchase, prepare, and cook nourishing food. It is so much easier and faster to buy packaged mixes, precooked, and frozen items instead of combining fresh ingredients containing the necessary nutrients in sufficient quantity and balance to maintain optimum health.

This fast-food habit results in a vicious circle. Empty calories cause chronic hunger, which many people attempt to allay by indulging in frequent between-meal snacks, which also lack adequate nourishment. Consequently, people often lack energy, are listless and uninterested in whatever they are doing, are too tired to engage in any form of exercise, and are content to waste time and energy on useless sedentary pursuits.

Baba recommends eating as much raw food as possible to replenish the energy that is used in all the varied activities and responsibilities attendant on daily living. He cautions us again and again to remember that we are not the body. On the other hand, he encourages us to take good care of it.

The Sense of Sight and Waste of Food

It is a well-known fact that when food is appealing to the eye, the very sight of it will whet the appetite and make it more readily assimilable because the digestive juices necessary for adequate digestion are thus stimulated. In the case of people who are ill and have lost their appetite, food that is attractively presented is much more likely to arouse their interest in eating it. It is an art to arrange a plate of food so that color and design are as pleasing to the eye as flavorful entrées are to the palate. Cooks in Japan are noted for their esthetic designs, and in many restaurants in that country artfully arranged trays of food will be placed in the window to tempt customers to eat there.

The sense of sight is a useful tool with which to determine whether an item of food is fresh or stale, and therefore wise to eat or better to avoid. It is when the sight of food stimulates greed, or an addiction, that it can lead to waste. The well-known saying, "Your eyes are bigger than your stomach," succinctly describes the tendency to buy more or ingest more of a particular food or drink than is actually needed to allay hunger or thirst. Moderation is the key, for as Baba repeatedly points out, "Food is the antidote for hunger; drink is the cure for thirst." This implies that anything beyond those basic needs spells waste.

As with waste of money through the sense of sight, waste of food often results from watching displays of delicious-looking meals shown in television commercials where advertisers use all the skills at their disposal to excite the appetite of viewers, which invariably results in overindulgence in those items. Some people find it very hard to resist the sight of bubbling entrées or mouth-watering desserts being displayed, which can—in only a few minutes—cause all their best intentions to collapse.

Similar lures are contained in the advertisements in magazines and other periodicals, where items of food are shown in lifelike colors to appeal to the most jaded palates. Imagine how hard it must be for those on a strict diet to have their favorite foods flashed in front of their eyes when they least expect it, and, consequently, when they are most vulnerable.

Preoccupation with food can stem from either positive or negative overemphasis in childhood, usually by parents. For many people, food has been associated with comfort, satisfaction, and security, and in some cases it has even substituted for the love every child needs and craves, when that was lacking. Food has also been used by parents as a bribe, a reward, even at times as a threat or, when purposely withdrawn, as a form of punishment. This early training can lead to future questionable attitudes about food. Another unfortunate practice of some parents is to stuff their babies and young children with food for fear they are not eating enough on their own to grow strong and develop properly. This tendency often causes a habit of overeating and an eventual weight problem, with all the attendant unpleasant consequences, later in life. If they are offered nourishing food, children generally choose to eat what their bodies need.

The Sense of Hearing and Waste of Food

As with the waste of money, television and radio commercials are the two most potent persuaders in waste of food through the sense of hearing, whether they lead to the decision to buy items containing too little food value, or those foods that can only add to the problem of addiction, overweight, and other allied problems.

Hearing foods described in glowing terms can rouse a desire so strong that it overcomes the firmest resolve to abstain from the very items that have already caused an addiction or other health problems. Those who suffer from overeating are particularly prone to have their resolution rapidly dissolve when hearing about the very foods they know from experience cause their downfall.

Alcoholics Anonymous suggest that when people become aware that they have a drinking problem, their only recourse is to refrain from partaking of any intoxicants. The same rule can also apply to those who are addicted to certain foods that they know cause excess weight. Hearing how delicious such foods are—either over the radio, on television commercials, or from friends and acquaintances—is often fatal to the success of the chosen self-help program embarked upon. Similarly, hearing about special sales on food as advertised by stores or restaurants can entice the mind to take advantage of the imagined bargains and lead people to acquire excessive amounts of a particular item, or indulge in unwise choices, simply because they sound so tasty or offer such a saving of money.

Many people use food as a topic of conversation, and, interestingly enough, this practice seems to occur more often in restaurants where friends gather to enjoy a meal together. So many times the conversations overheard at nearby tables are dominated by the subject of food and the menus of other favorite restaurants. This is especially true if any of the diners have recently "eaten their way through Europe," as some travelers express it.

The Senses of Taste and Smell and Waste of Food

There is a great contrast between eating to allay hunger and thirst—in which case we retain control—and allowing a particular substance to be in control of us, such as when we find ourselves grabbing, gulping, or having our thoughts always filled with the desire for a favorite delicacy. Our senses of taste and smell are the ones that most readily lead the mind to crave food or drink to excess.

In many cases, eating habits have been established in infancy. Since we all tend to follow the patterns with which our parents have programmed us, we develop habits on an unconscious level, which means we are not always aware that we are continuing to follow them. As no one can change a habit until and unless he or she becomes aware of it, we need to observe the ways our senses of smell and taste tempt us to overindulge ourselves on certain items of food and drink, or on any other substances taken into the body that appeal to those two senses.

Individual preferences and aversions vary considerably. To one person the smell or taste of coffee can be most alluring, while another may react to it with a feeling of distaste. Many people thoroughly enjoy the smell and taste of peanuts and pickles, both of which make me feel quite ill. The same applies to the smell of tobacco. To some people the smell of a cigarette, a cigar, or a pipe being smoked nearby can produce a feeling of nausea, while others may be overcome by a craving to smoke, particularly if they have a history of addiction to smoking.

Wine also appeals to these two senses of smell and taste. Wine tasters are employed specifically to select the wines they consider to have the desired taste and bouquet in any given variety. Those they finally approve, of course, become the most sought after and expensive. Likewise, tea tasters are employed to give their opinion of various types of tea according to how they taste and smell, which again are priced accordingly.

The process of observing our own reactions is not designed to force us to act like a policeman and prevent us or others from enjoying food and drink. Rather, it is the waste of any of these substances caused by their smell or taste that needs to be addressed and eliminated. There is such a vast selection of foods and beverages available, especially in the Western countries, that everyone has his or her own particular temptations, so it is necessary to observe which items are capable of luring each person to certain foods that can lead to waste of some kind. To list all the possibilities would be tedious and of no avail, as we are all so different and we each have our own craving for specific things.

The Sense of Touch and Waste of Food

The many different textures of food and drink can exert their power to entice a person to buy too much, to buy unwisely, or to eat or drink more than is necessary to allay the appetite or assuage the thirst. Preferences differ as widely regarding the textures of food as they do with taste. From a very early age even babies exhibit their likes and dislikes, not only of the taste but also of the way food feels to them. They show their approval or dislike of a particular item by smiling and smacking their lips, or making a grimace and spitting it out. Some prefer soft mushy food, while others like their food to be firm and crunchy. Some like hot food rather than cold, while others prefer the reverse. There are limitless variations that attract or repel.

In addition to texture there is the effect of the different tastes such as sweet, salty, sour, spicy, savory, or bitter, and how each of these flavors feels on the tongue and in the mouth. The way in which certain foods or drinks make us feel can also cause waste, if it leads to gluttony. Whatever tempts us to eat or drink more than we really need contributes to waste.

You are all too attached to what you can see.
When you turn from the world you discover me.
When you loosen attachments and attach to me
I can fill you full of ecstasy.

If you pay the price and are willing to work,
You will reach the goal in which I lurk.
I love you although you know it not.
You are my treasures that never rot.

I polish and carve you to fit my form.
You squirm and resist to fit the norm.
When you break out of your tight little shell
You'll enjoy the peace of which none can tell.

So come into my arms forever to stay
And roam no more, neither night nor day.
For here you are safe and can come to no harm
Like a ship in a harbor where all is calm.

Chapter 11

Waste of Time

I shall never forget how surprised I was when, in an interview devoted entirely to the Ceiling on Desires program, Baba pointed out that everyone in the entire world has exactly the same amount of time at his or her disposal. We all have just twenty-four hours each day to use for all the varied activities in our particular life. He added that if any part of it is wasted it is gone forever, never to be retrieved.

We are all prone to waste time without even realizing that we are doing so, simply because so many time-wasters have developed into habits over the years, and we all know how hard it is to break a habit once it is formed. So, just as we need to know how we use the available supply of money and food, we also need to clarify how we use time so that we can judge whether we may be wasting it in idle or meaningless pursuits.

It is obvious that most people need to spend the major portion of their time engaged in pursuing the career or occupation that enables them to support themselves and their families. This daily activity usually consumes about eight of the available twenty-four hours. However, even within the time devoted to some kind of gainful activity, there are many periods of wastefulness; a situation that needs to be examined.

But it is the less organized activities such as the daily routine of a housewife and mother, a writer or an artist, and other occupations where we are left pretty much to our own devices that allow plenty of opportunity to waste time. When there are no authority figures to act as supervisors, we need to be our own overseer, to make sure we are not wasting time without even being aware of doing so. As an aid in such a situation, many people find that making a list of the various tasks that need to be undertaken during the day clarifies the otherwise vague and often muddled schedule they face, which can cause them to waste time out of confusion or frustration. When time is better organized there will be more of it available to devote to leisure activities. However, it is during those times we are free from major tasks that many people find they are most inclined to indulge in activities that provide the minimum of fulfillment, which means time wasted.

Most people will agree that at certain times of the day they seem to be more alert, while at other times their energy level appears to plummet. Some will even go so far as to state that they are "night people" who prefer to stay up later at night and are reluctant to arise early in the morning. Others enjoy the daytime hours and awake each morning full of enthusiasm for whatever events the day ahead may hold for them. But these "day people" are ready to go to bed earlier in the evening than their night-loving friends or relatives. It is helpful to assess the best or worst periods of the day or night and plan the main work tasks around them to obtain the most benefit from the time available.

Baba has also mentioned that too many hours spent in sleep is a waste of time, especially if it is used as an escape from facing life and the problems to be solved; or if sleep is used to escape those tasks that have been labeled unpleasant or boring. Work, difficult relationships, or other problems should be addressed and resolved, rather than avoided by escaping into sleep.

Neither too much sleep nor too little is advisable. Individual needs differ according to our metabolism, so we should determine the proper amount of rest our body needs to be refreshed. Usually, the best way to regulate sleep is to try to ensure the same number of hours each night. This involves resisting the temptation to indulge in unnecessary activities that delay sleep and cause one to awaken still tired and unrefreshed. On the other hand, it is equally undesirable to be self-indulgent and sleep too much, which causes sluggishness.

Baba repeatedly states that the majority of people are prone to waste time in idle and meaningless activities, yet frequently say they do not have time for service, meditation, or other beneficial activities. It is very important to bring about a balance of work, exercise, diet, sleep, worship, and recreation in order to stay healthy in body, mind, and spirit. Baba has suggested for his devotees, "Of the twenty-four hours of the day, have six hours for your individual needs, six hours for the service of others, six hours for sleep, and six for dwelling in the presence of the Lord. Those six hours will endow you with the strength of steel."

But few people seem to realize that waste of time does not mean only waste of their own available amount of time, it also includes the waste of other people's time, in which case it is the same as stealing from them. How can we be guilty of wasting other people's time? When we are late for an appointment of any kind, we waste not only our own time but also the time of the person or people we have kept waiting for our arrival. While we delay, we are also causing those who await us unnecessary stress, whether they are friends, business associates, children we are picking up from school, or those employed in service activities, such as hairdressers, doctors, dentists and other professionals, or anyone who has regular appointments to keep.

Many people have been irritated by being forced to waste time by having to wait to be given attention because another person was thoughtless enough to be late for his or her appointment, which makes all the succeeding ones late due to such selfishness. It is especially annoying if the person in question has the reputation for always being late. The same is true of any family member who consistently keeps the other members waiting while he or she attends to last-minute details that should have been allotted sufficient time earlier, in order to avoid the delay. I have had many children tell me how nervous and neglected they felt when they were not picked up from nursery school or kindergarten at the correct time but were left waiting for their parent long after the other children had departed.

Of course, there are unexpected delays such as a traffic jam, an accident, a plane arriving later than scheduled, and other occurrences that are no fault of the victims. It is those people who make a practice of being late and of keeping others waiting who need to ask themselves the reason for this wasteful habit. Was it caused during childhood by parents who were always hurrying them? Is it a bid for attention or power over others to counteract feelings of insecurity, frustration, inadequacy, or low self-esteem? It is definitely a sign of selfishness and lack of consideration for others, whatever the original cause may have been. But whatever the reason it is still a waste of time, whether their own or someone else's. If the latter is the case, it is no different than stealing something belonging to another person.

What other thieves of time are there? Worrying looms large on the list. It has absolutely no value whatsoever and devours time that could be used in purposeful pursuits. It acts like the wheels of a car spinning in sand that prevents the vehicle from proceeding on its journey, thus delaying progress of any kind.

Talking interminably about one's problems to other people, either in person or over the telephone, is another time-waster that prevents both parties from using the time involved to better advantage. Discussing a problem in order to try to solve it can be helpful; it is the habit of talking in circles and going nowhere that wastes the time of both the listeners and the talkers.

Daydreaming is another useless activity that many people indulge in to excess. Everyone needs a certain amount of relaxed time to allow the nervous system to return to normal after a period of great activity, whether physical, mental, or emotional. But, instead of frittering away time in idle dreaming, worrying, or nervousness it is preferable to calm the mind and ask for input from that wiser part of us—the High Self—which can provide inspiration when asked for help. Then the time used will result in genuine benefit instead of waste. For the more we turn within to consult the Higher Consciousness available to all of us the more truly successful our lives will be, as they will come more and more under the influence of the true Self instead of the ego with its multitude of desires.

The Sense of Sight and Waste of Time

How do the eyes lead the mind to attach itself to sights that result in a waste of time? Any activity is a waste of time unless it benefits in some way the person concerned and/or others. Some of the chief time-wasters through the sense of sight are watching television, home videos, motion pictures, and plays, if the programs present to the viewer little positive input in return for the time spent watching them. It is absolutely essential to evaluate what possible benefit may be derived in order to determine if the time spent will be well used or wasted.

Many forms of so-called entertainment that portray salacious or violent themes can have a negative impact on the viewers. Like food, whatever else is taken into the body through any of the senses is also internalized and can have the effect of elevating and inspiring the recipients or overstimulating them and stirring up negative emotions by encouraging them to identify themselves with the least admirable instincts.

In addition to watching time-wasting programs, excessive reading is another time-waster through the sense of sight, whether books, newspapers, magazines, or other periodicals are preferred. This is especially true if the material also contains subject matter that could have a negative impact and result in violent or destructive behavior, or if reading is simply used as an escape from attending to daily duties or family relationships. Unfortunately, many people read the newspaper from cover to cover, paying special attention to the more lurid articles on gang violence, murders, sexual exploits, and other sensational subjects. Many unnecessary hours are wasted in such idle and uninspiring reading.

The Sense of Hearing and Waste of Time

Many of the same ways in which money and food can be wasted through the sense of hearing also apply to the waste of time. These include the hours many people waste in watching television programs, listening to the radio, attending certain plays, lectures, and seminars, if the content is likely to have a disturbing effect on the mind or emotions, or is merely inconsequential and useless rather than edifying.

But there are other ways by which our ears involve us in time-wasting pursuits. These include indulging in idle conversation—either in person or over the telephone— especially if it involves gossip or maligning other people by either of the two parties participating.

Lately, there has been a great deal of discussion on the subject of different types of pollution, and more attention is now being given to pollution caused by noise whether it is due to a fleet of planes flying overhead, rush-hour traffic, heavy hammering and other sounds related to building projects or repairs to other structures, dogs barking, motorcycles being started, radios, stereos, and television sets blaring, babies crying, children screeching, or even people with unusually loud voices talking continuously. All these can result in a waste of time if they distract us from pursuing the task in which we are engaged. In many workplaces noise pollution is being recognized as a factor in loss of time, and in many organizations soft music or "white sound" is being introduced to offset this hazard.

But we ourselves have a responsibility regarding the waste of our own time. It can mean being willing to exert ourselves to eliminate such distractions as much as possible without unduly inconveniencing others. Sometimes it takes courage to bring an instance of noise pollution to the attention of a person in authority and request a remedy for it.

Often direct intervention is not possible or wise, so other protective methods need to be resorted to. I happen to have extremely sensitive hearing, so I have learned from experience always to carry cotton balls or rubber earplugs to use whenever I find myself unexpectedly in a situation where I have no control over the noise.

Pollution of all kinds causes stress, which in turn causes not only waste of time but also waste of energy. So by avoiding it as much as possible, without being fanatical and creating a problem for others, we can reduce the stress we all carry and thus save the time it can cause us to waste.

The Senses of Smell and Taste and Waste of Time

Again, as with other types of waste, these two senses belong together as possible time-wasters. For instance, when we smell coffee being brewed, bread being baked, or any other aroma that pleases our sense of smell it can make us spend time that could be better used in other ways than indulging our senses of smell and taste.

Another way time can be wasted is in preparing and cooking food. Many people enjoy the process because of the pleasant smells that permeate the air and hold out promise of a mouth-watering repast. If this activity uses up too much time that could be used more beneficially for other activities, it is time wasted. Both gourmets and gourmands are liable to waste inordinate amounts of time in relishing food and wine. However, this is not intended to imply that we should eat too quickly and rush through our meals, unconscious of the whole process of digestion, which requires us to be relaxed and undisturbed while eating. It is only the waste of time expended in the process that should be eliminated.

The Sense of Touch and Waste of Time

The sense of touch is useful in providing insight into how something either outside or inside our body makes us feel. It is an indicator of what has a pleasing effect and what produces pain or discomfort.

Some people like to feel stimulated, while others react with pleasure to feeling relaxed or sedated. Baba often mentions the three *gunas* and their action in human beings thus: *rajasic* substances or experiences have a stimulating effect; *tamasic* influences tend to make people sluggish or lethargic; while *sathwic* conditions create a calm, yet alert, state. He instructs us that we need to remain as much as possible in the *sathwic* state and not let our monkey minds persuade us to become attached to either of the other two, or swing back and forth between them.

If we allow ourselves to be controlled by the sense of touch by becoming attached or addicted to things that make us feel good, we can easily be led into wasting time by indulging this sense, in which case it gains control over us instead of our retaining control over it and maintaining a balanced state of being.

Drugs, liquor, sex, and all kinds of stimulants and sedatives can cause a waste of time and even more waste when, in addition, they render us less capable of living and working effectively. If we are overstimulated we are not in control of a situation, of our thoughts, or of our emotions and actions. Likewise, if we are drugged into a stupor, we are not able to react appropriately and responsibly in work, relationships, or any other aspect of life.

Only when we are relaxed but not sedated, and are alert but not too excited can we be fully conscious of the inner direction of the High Self. Our aim should be to avoid the two extremes and strive for a modicum of balance in our lives. Anything that either overstimulates or dulls our perception is capable of exerting undue control over us and can lead to a waste of time. For instance, surfing—a popular pastime (especially in southern California)—if indulged in to excess becomes an addiction and acts like a drug. It makes the enthusiast feel good since it combines excitement and near-hypnosis. It can be an excellent exercise if the surfers retain control and not waste time they can ill afford to lose, however good it makes them feel.

Working out in a gymnasium, aerobics, marathons, and all the other popular physical activities can also become time-wasters if they exert so much control over the athletes that they become drugged or obsessed and, as a result, neglect other important areas of their lives. We have all heard the jokes about golf widows whose husbands indulge their passion for their preferred sport to the exclusion of other interests, including time spent with their families, because it makes them feel so good.

Sunbathing to excess is another time-wasting activity if it tempts the sun-lover to spend too many hours in the sun. An added hazard is the danger of skin cancer. Too much sun can change swiftly from giving pleasure to causing pain if too much time is wasted in pursuing it.

These are only a few examples. We all need to become aware of our own time-wasters and check to make sure that they are not causing us to waste time on activities that appeal to our sense of touch or feeling. Balance is essential to prevent the sense of touch from luring us to indulge in wasting time.

I am the breath of your life,
I am the sound of your song,
I am the heat of your sun,
So what can go wrong?

You must have no fear,
For I am within;
Go forth with gladness,
Filled to the brim.

Let my love shine forth
On all those you meet
While on a journey,
Or as a man on the street . . .

You must love me and cradle me
And make me your own,
And I will be with you
Wherever you roam.

I am deep inside you
And can never be lost,
So accept my presence
And don't count the cost.

I will be with you
From morning to night,
To fill you forever
With my shining light.

So rock me and cradle me
And sing me a song,
And you will discover
You cannot go wrong.

Chapter 12

Waste of Energy

Unlike time, everyone does not have an equal amount of energy. It varies a great deal in different individuals, even from birth. So it behooves each one of us to make sure to use whatever amount we are blessed with in pursuits that are as productive as possible, and in this way avoid wasting our precious allowance.

One of the most effective ways to reduce waste of energy is to overcome the habit of control that is fast becoming the chief cause of heart attacks, ulcers, strokes, nervous breakdowns, suicides, and many other problems directly resulting from stress. Stress is invariably caused by compulsion to control situations, other people, our own lives, or anything else. We may be unconscious of this acute need to control our environment until the resulting stress forces us to become aware of its cause, which is our own attitude.

As a start in alleviating this situation, it is important to realize that it is not necessary to drive ourselves to overachieve or to strive for perfection. Such needless effort is not only a waste of energy, but creates tension that can strain the nervous system and eventually leave insufficient energy with which to perform even the most simple tasks.

If, instead of forcing issues with the mind and will, we can learn to let go and allow the High Self to accomplish the various tasks through us, we will discover that the tension disappears and we are able to undertake and complete everything we have to do with plenty of energy to spare. This surplus energy can then be utilized for such activities as meditation, exercise, service to those less fortunate than ourselves, and all the things we complain that we have no time or energy to pursue because we are too tired.

Baba points out that "thoughts originate in the mind, they express themselves through words, and are materialized through deeds." So he suggests that we "dedicate every thought, word, and deed to God by effacing our will, accepting His will, and leaving all initiation of activity to His prompting, all execution to His direction, and all consequences to His plan." As an aid in letting go in this way, every morning in meditation we can sincerely ask the High Self to:

1. **THINK** through us all day. This will help our minds stay alert and free to be used for what is really necessary. We can then relax and follow the inner direction, which we will soon begin to detect. In this way we will accomplish much more than we were ever able to before, with far less stress or effort on our part, which will result in the saving of both time and energy.

2. **FEEL** through us all day. This will help us avoid being tempted to spend our precious supply of energy in useless sentimentality, or even the more wasteful negative emotions such as anger, fear, hate, jealousy, envy, and all the rest. Baba has stated that one bout of anger uses more energy than we receive from the food we eat over a period of three months. So, anger is not only a waste of energy but also of money, food, and time, all of which are also forms of energy.

3. **SPEAK** through us all day. This will help us reduce the huge expenditure of energy when we speak too forcefully, or our speech is motivated by anger or a determination to get our own way, or from the desire to control another person. It has been proved that the human voice can be— and often is used as—one of the most effective ways of gaining control over people, especially if they are suscep-

tible to hypnosis or domination by others. Baba says that "speech is a great gift, for it is the natural weapon of human beings. Animals and other species have horns, tusks, talons, teeth, and other weapons with which to protect themselves. But only man has speech, which, if used sweetly, is the greatest weapon of all."

4. **ACT** through us all day. This will minimize the waste of energy expended in unnecessary activities and will help us withdraw our control, so that our actions are relaxed and flowing instead of tense and controlling.

5. Send Its **LOVE** through us all day to flow through our thoughts, feelings, words, and deeds to conserve the greatest amount of energy for use in more profitable pursuits. Everything we do that is not accompanied by love is a waste of some kind of energy. In this way we can restrain our monkey minds from flitting here and there in search of objects on which to alight, like butterflies seeking honey, and cease being tempted to commit any kind of waste. For our thoughts, feelings, words, and actions will be determined by the High Self, which wastes absolutely nothing as It is always in perfect balance. This way of living will allow us to accomplish another of the tasks Baba has set us; namely, to make our thoughts, words, and deeds all the same instead of having each one express different attitudes. Then we can be free and open, with nothing hidden, devious, or manipulative.

In addition to our own supply of energy, we should also avoid wasting other types such as water, electricity, gasoline, and so forth to ensure that we have enough available for our use. We can also help the current world problem by conserving the planet's natural resources. This would include avoiding waste of paper in an effort to preserve the forests, which are rapidly being denuded to meet the increasing demand for innumerable wood products being used in all parts of the world.

Water is another form of energy, and with the drought in many parts of the world we need to be careful not to waste it by leaving faucets running, flushing toilets more often than is absolutely necessary, taking long showers or too many baths, and using more water than we really need when watering the garden, running the dishwasher and washing machine, or engaging in other activities using water.

Recycling cans and bottles is another way to control waste. For more ideas on this subject, we can contact various local agencies who have worked out programs outlining practical ways we can all help in these projects.

The Sense of Sight and Waste of Energy

The eyes are the most sensitive organs in the body, and we all tend to overwork and overstimulate them by expecting them to serve us indefinitely with little or no care from us. Eyestrain causes tremendous waste of energy because the eyes are directly connected to the nervous system. When the eyes are overstimulated or tired the whole person is depleted of energy.

Today we expect our eyes to serve us in ways that were never dreamed of before this century. We take for granted that they will continue to read fine print for long hours, and we are not always careful to make sure the lighting is adequate. We expect them to watch a computer screen without rest periods, watch television programs for hours at a time, and subject them to numerous other uses that cause eyestrain and impose a severe drain on our energy.

To avoid this problem we need to alternate physical activities to allow the eyes to relax periodically by engaging in tasks that use the larger muscles of the body to give the sensitive ones in the eyes a rest. After a period of close work it is also advisable to do something that requires the eyes to look further into the distance, thereby using different muscles. This simple exercise can quickly ease strained eyes that have been forced to concentrate on close work for too long a time. Eye muscles, like all other muscles, need regular exercise but not if it means using more energy than is actually available on any single activity. Many things we do cause a kind of hypnosis that in turn causes us to be unconscious of the fact that we are wasting energy. We become so involved in whatever we are doing that we lose our perspective.

Another way the sense of sight can cause waste of energy is when we allow the eye to attach us to the desire for something they have seen. This prompts us to use energy to attain it by whatever means necessary, such as driving to a store. Or we become so frustrated if we are not able to procure it that we waste energy in useless anger, worry, regret, and any of the many other reactions to unrequited desires. More energy is used in regret than in active sports, for it eats away at our mental equilibrium.

The Sense of Hearing and Waste of Energy

Any of the senses that are used to the point of exhaustion cause a drain on our energy. Just as we can experience eyestrain from abusing the eyes by overworking them, we can also deplete our energy by overloading the ears with discordant sounds. This is particularly noticeable after listening to any loud noise over long periods, and we begin to feel tired as a result of our overstimulated nerves. The current habit among children and young adults of listening incessantly to loud music has the effect of dulling their hearing, in some cases to an alarming extent. Anything that stimulates the nervous system produces stress on the entire body, which in turn lowers the energy available to the person concerned.

Experiments have been set up to examine the effect of sound on the growth of plants with most interesting results. It was found that when plants are exposed to melodious sounds they thrive and grow taller and stronger, and they appear to exude an air of well-being. But when harsh sounds, such as those heard in rock-and-roll music are broadcast to them they do not grow as fast and are not nearly as healthy, and some even die. If plants react negatively to sound, imagine how much more acutely it must affect human beings and reduce their energy!

We are all free to choose whether we want to take a chance and lower our energy, and therefore our ability to function well, by exposing our ears to jarring sounds; or we can choose to avoid listening to sounds we already know will cause a reduction in our efficiency by depleting our energy, such as people complaining in a loud voice, angrily shouting and screaming about some real or imagined wrong, or any other disquieting assault on our ears.

We all need periods of quiet to allow our nervous system as well as our ears to rest, but it is a very real necessity for those who are exposed to an extreme amount of noise pollution during the day while they are at work. Any activity that is continued without surcease is exhausting to the nerves, which need a respite to return to normal after a period of stress.

The Senses of Taste and Smell and Waste of Energy

The food we eat is our main source of energy. We need to ascertain whether we are giving our bodies the kind of food that will provide the optimum amount of energy for use in our daily life. Sugar is one of the items that can cause the energy level in many people to fluctuate violently, resulting in repeated shocks to the whole system. This reaction is especially true for those who suffer from hypoglycemia, or low blood sugar, a condition in which the sugar level in the blood reaches too high a peak after the intake of sugar, followed almost immediately by a drastic drop in the sugar level.

The majority of people enjoy sweet foods and drinks. However, many people are addicted to the surge of energy that sugar temporarily provides. Diabetics have the opposite reaction to sugar intake and need to monitor the amount of sugar they ingest to prevent the coma that can result from a sudden extreme reduction of insulin. Interestingly enough, there are indications that if hypoglycemia is not brought under control it can slip over into diabetes. Surprisingly, the most effective way to control it is by the same method diabetics are forced to use, which is reduction of the ingestion of sugar in any form.

In some cases of alcoholism an underlying cause is found to be an imbalance in the handling of sugar, even though it may be hidden. Also, Baba has warned us that white sugar is one of the causes of cancer due to the lye used in the bleaching process.

We can take responsibility for preserving a balance by bearing in mind that the monkey mind needs to be controlled and not allowed to grab foods or drinks that are loaded with sugar just because they taste so good. The taste lasts only a few minutes while the deleterious effects are more lasting and serious.

The Sense of Touch and Waste of Energy

Not everything that feels good to the touch is necessarily beneficial. Again, it is a case for moderation. Too much of anything can cause problems, but so can too little. By watching our energy level we can determine how much of something is too much for our personal tolerance and how much is too little for our comfort.

For instance, many people enjoy being massaged, but if they indulge in this pleasure too often it can become an addiction and steal not only energy but time and money. The same principle applies to exercise; the right amount enhances our energy, whereas more than we can handle physically may waste energy and become useless repetition.

Sunbathing feels good, but it too can cause a drop in the energy level and a feeling of sluggishness if indulged in for too long or too often. Long hot baths have a similarly debilitating effect, even though initially they can be very relaxing.

Lovemaking and sex is perhaps the human activity that can have the most energizing effect on the participants, but if repeated too often it has the opposite effect, depleting the energy of one or both partners. It is all a matter of discovering the correct balance between too much of a good thing and too little. These are merely a few suggestions that can be augmented by each person's individual experience.

Beloved Baba take my heart
And through it pour your love.
Beloved Baba fill my head
With wisdom from above.

Beloved Baba let my tongue
Speak only what you will.
Beloved Baba use my hands
Your wishes to fulfill.

Beloved Baba lead my feet
The dharmic path to tread.
And above all else, dear Baba,
Grant my will to yours be wed.

Chapter 13

The Monkey Mind—
Thinking, Feeling, Speaking, and Acting

Baba's advice is to watch the following:

W	Watch your Words
A	Watch your Actions
T	Watch your Thoughts
C	Watch your Character
H	Watch your Heart

The mind should be the master not only over the five senses, but over the functions of thinking, feeling, speaking, and acting. Otherwise, any one or all four of them can gain power and become the master instead of useful servants. We can be dominated by our thoughts, by our feelings, by our words, and by our actions if any or all of these succeed in compelling us to follow their lead.

The Monkey Mind and Thinking

We have all had the experience of literally being bedeviled by thoughts about something to such a degree that we find we are incapable of stopping the process. Eventually we become so attached to this situation—and the thoughts possess us to such an extent—that we are quite helpless to break free from their control. We have all heard people say, "I simply cannot get such and such out of my mind however hard I try, and it is driving me crazy." We have probably been in that position ourselves at some time or other. This slavery to our own thoughts imprisons us just as effectively as a jail constructed from bricks or cement.

Thoughts tend to go around and around in the mind like a squirrel in a cage with no apparent way out of the predicament. They appear to be real or valid, yet they are actually only thoughts with as yet no solidity, and are invariably our own limited thoughts at that, so they can very easily be erroneous.

In the early days, on the more universal or world level, it was thought that the earth was flat and that anyone who ventured too far in any direction would quite likely fall off into space. When more accurate methods to determine the shape of the planet were discovered, showing it to be spherical instead of flat, people continued to cling to the old belief despite the new evidence to the contrary, and they persecuted those who had presented the new idea.

Many wars have been fought between those who held differing beliefs or ideas, both sides continuing to be equally determined to prove that their belief was the correct one. Therefore, the group that thought otherwise must be wrong and should either be punished or eradicated. Of course, such an impasse is not limited solely to groups or nations. It exists between individuals at all levels of society. It stems from the foolish and shortsighted need of trying to prove ourselves to be right and concluding that anyone who disagrees with us must necessarily be wrong, forgetting that several different points of view are possible.

Innumerable similar situations have arisen throughout the long history of the world, the tragedy being that only rarely is either side completely right or entirely wrong, since it is all relative. No one has access to the whole truth about anything at any particular time. We each have our own small part but foolishly and egotistically believe we have the whole, and when it appears to differ from someone else's piece we are so certain that we have the entire picture that we are equally sure that the other person must be wrong.

The story of the three blind men who were asked to describe an elephant illustrates this point very well. They all approached the animal and each one put out his hand to touch it in order to determine its shape. One man's hand came in contact with its trunk, and, thinking he had hold of the entire creature, he described it as long and tubular like a snake. Another of the men took hold of one of its ears and described the elephant as flat and pliable. The third man touched its leg and declared that the animal was large and round and firm and resembled a tree trunk. As can be seen from this story they were all correctly reporting their individual views, but they failed to realize that each one had described only one part of the whole elephant, which was much greater than the sum of the three parts.

Strongly held beliefs fall into this category. There are some subjects about which we may have very strong thoughts without ever attempting to ascertain whether we really do believe them to be true or even useful at the present time. Many concepts were valid in a certain era when they were timely and helpful but have no further relevance now, yet we still cling to them as if they guaranteed some kind of security, like a raft in a rough sea.

It is necessary to ask ourselves repeatedly, "Do I really believe this or that and is it applicable now? Does it hamper my progress or free me for action?" If a particular belief is no longer valid it should be dropped. As we mature, many cherished beliefs become obsolete and are a hindrance instead of a help.

As changes occur in the world, particularly those resulting from all the new discoveries, inventions, and methods of working, the old outmoded concepts that are no longer useful should be discarded to stop our monkey minds from continuing to hold on to them, when letting go of them would set us free from their control over us. Baba's suggestion to accomplish this task is, "Your first duty is to abandon. Abandon all the theories you cherish, the doctrines you hold dear, the systems of knowledge that have cluttered your brain, the preferences you have accumulated, the pursuit of fame, fortune, scholarship, superiority. These are all material, objective. Enter into the objective world after becoming aware of the Atma. Then you will realize that all is the play of the Atma."

The Monkey Mind and Feeling

In a similar way we can also be dominated by our feelings. Sadness, guilt, worry, jealousy, envy, anger, and many other emotions can gain such control over us that we are rendered helpless in their grip, yet cannot take the obvious steps to extricate ourselves and be free from their control simply by letting go of them. We are just as pathetic as the monkey with its fist trapped inside the bottle, when all it needs to do is let go of the fruit or nuts it clutches to free its arm from its temporary prison. We too can stop being a slave to our feelings.

Some people seem to derive a sense of gratification from entertaining negative feelings that, notwithstanding their damaging effect, stir up excitement and provide welcome relief from boredom and depression. Negative emotions can also have a stimulating action on the adrenal glands with a resulting rush of energy that provides us with a sense of physical well-being and snaps us out of the previous bored or depressed mood. However, satisfaction derived from such feelings is short-lived, and, like the proverbial scorpion with a sting in its tail, it can end up poisoning us with our own venom; what Shakespeare called, "Being hoist with his own petard," or wounded with his own weapon.

So, feelings of anger, resentment, envy, jealousy, and a host of similar emotions can gain mastery over us if we allow them to develop beyond a certain point before letting go of them, after which they become too strong for that to be possible. Such destructive emotions all have their source in thwarted desires. We need to trace each one back to the desire that spawned it and remember that if we can let go of the desire and be mindful of the saying, "Thy will, not mine, be done," we will be free from its control over our emotions.

Self-pity—couched in such phrases as, "Everyone else has this or that, so why don't I?" or, "No one else has to work as hard as I do and with so little appreciation," or, "Why do I have to do this or that while other people have such an easy life?"—can assume such proportions that it takes over control of our feelings and we discover that we are helpless to escape its domination.

The Monkey Mind and Speaking

Baba points out that the tongue has not one but two functions. He says, "While the eye, the ear, and the nose serve as instruments of knowledge about one particular characteristic of nature, the tongue makes itself available for two purposes: to judge taste and to utter words and syllables of communication. So control the tongue with double care since it can harm you in two ways."

We often speak without first considering what we are about to say and the possible effect it may have on the listeners. If only we could remember to pause before we impulsively launch into an avalanche of words, we would be better able to put an end to the monkey mind's attachment to our function of speech.

Many people only talk to show how much they know and to prove to themselves as well as to others that they are special or superior in some way instead of attempting to exchange ideas, discoveries, knowledge, or facts. By holding on tightly to their imaginary importance and proclaiming their prowess to those who are willing to listen, they become imprisoned by their attachment to their own words.

A similar situation can be observed in those who lie about their feats or exaggerate them by boasting. Lies generate more lies until we are buried beneath a heavy pile of our own fabrications. We cannot escape unless we are willing to face the situation into which our behavior has led us and to seek help to dispel the feelings of insecurity that forced us to magnify our worth by bragging about real or imaginary achievements.

The Monkey Mind and Action

Our monkey mind influences our actions both on the conscious and unconscious levels. An example of the way the monkey mind may be attached to action can be observed in those people who are engaged in constant activity and never seem to be able to relax and be quiet for any length of time. They are literally addicted to nonstop activity and feel utterly insecure if they have to stop their frenzied motion due to illness, an accident, or some other reason.

It is easy to see that anything we cannot stop doing can make us aware of those activities to which we have become so attached that they control us instead of our being in control of what we do. Workaholics fall into this category since the work they do to excess controls them, and they become as trapped by it as the monkey with its arm stuck inside the bottle. Like the monkey, we have the key to our prison in our own hands. We can let go of whatever it is we are holding on to instead of bemoaning the fact that we are helplessly imprisoned—not by someone else, but by something we ourselves have caused.

What is the reason for such excessive activity? It is usually to avoid having to face ourselves, observe our faults, and put our lives into better order. For many people, having their attention completely distracted by frenzied activity leaves no time to think about anything else, including themselves or their behavior.

A simple formula has proved to be most useful in training the monkey mind to let go of whatever it is holding on to that eventually entraps it. It is to remember at the beginning of each day to ask Baba—who represents our true identity—to think through us, feel through us, speak through us, act through us, and especially to love through us all day long. If we can surrender these functions then, like Hanuman, we will become the servant of Rama or the Self we really are.

You are all my fingers and thumbs
You are all my toes and my feet.
You are all my heart and my head
Through whom I'll perform many feats.

Relax and allow me to work
In any way that I will
To help all those who are sad
And many of those who are ill.

Be not afraid of my power.
It is always directed by me.
You will merely be my tool
From now to eternity.

Chapter 14

The Monkey Mind Blames the Pot

Baba warns us thus, "Do not condemn the mind as a monkey. It is a fine instrument with which you can win either liberation or bondage." He also says, "The monkey that cannot pull out its clenched fist from the narrow neck of the pot lays blame on the pot or the maker of the pot. But, if only it would release its hold on the peanuts it has grasped in that fist, then it could easily take its hand out. The fault lies in itself. No one thrust its hand into the pot or forced the monkey to grab the nuts. It has become the victim of its own greed."

We are all like the monkey who blames the inert pot for its plight, when the monkey alone was responsible for its capture. It is so much easier and less threatening to cast the blame for our problems on to other people, such as our parents and their influence on us, our friends or enemies, our job—including our boss and coworkers—our siblings, our financial status, the circumstances of our birth, and all the thousands of other hooks on which we have tried to hang the blame for our problems.

But like the monkey we alone are to blame for our present situation, which is due either to our actions in past lives or in the current one. We have trapped ourselves whether we like to accept that fact or choose to deny it, for the law of action and reaction does not deviate or admit exceptions. So we are the only ones who can expedite our escape from the trap of our own making. Instead of blaming anything or anyone other than ourselves for our plight, we should take responsibility for our own actions and mistakes, both past and present, and stop avoiding the issue by feeling sorry for ourselves. Certainly, far more effective benefits will accrue if we do so.

Another method we all use to avoid putting our own lives in order is to project our faults and weaknesses on to others by busily criticizing and blaming them for the very blemishes we ourselves are guilty of possessing. I recall a little saying I often heard during my childhood: "Those who live in glass houses should never throw stones." As with so many other pithy sayings I did not fully understand its meaning, and as no one explained it to me it was absorbed into my subconscious mind along with the rest of the undigested or unprocessed bits of wisdom, ready to emerge into the light of consciousness at an appropriate time. Now I realize that it meant that it is usually much easier and more pleasant to sit in judgment of someone else rather than to expend the time and effort required to uncover and eradicate the blots in ourselves.

Another quotation that has assumed more meaning in the light of Baba's teachings is, "Judge not that ye be not judged. . . . Why beholdest thou the mote that is in thy brothers eye, but considerest not the beam that is in thine own eye?" (Matthew 7:1, 3). Everyone who has visited Baba in his ashram will have experienced the extreme discomfort of finding oneself in a situation that seems to have been uncannily designed to stir up all the negative reactions and feelings that were thought to have been safely buried out of sight, even from our own sight!

Baba has said that he deliberately uses certain people to teach others whatever they need to learn. For example, I remember one woman who was at the ashram during one of our early visits. Her behavior around Baba so shocked many of the devotees that we wondered why Baba continued to grant her privileges in spite of her actions. It was very hard for some of the young people to understand why she received so much attention from Baba while they, who were trying to abide by the rules of the ashram, were not being given as much as a glance from him during *darshan*. So one of the members of the organization asked Baba the reason why he overlooked her questionable behavior and appeared to be condoning it, explaining the effect this situation was having on some of the young people. Baba merely smiled and nodded his head as he told the man that he used this woman to stir up all the jealousy and envy hidden in many of the devotees who did not admit to harboring such emotions. He appears to be demonstrating that we all have problems, but only when we are aware of having them can we admit to them and let go of them. When we pretend to be perfect and without fault and project our own imperfections on to others by criticizing them for the very problems we have ourselves, we need to be jolted into recognizing our own blemishes, for they are the only ones we can relinquish.

Chapter 15

The Monkey Mind
and the Ashram Virus

Everyone who has traveled to India to visit Baba has become aware of the various infections and other illnesses that are to be found in all such crowded places. These often act as a cleansing agent to hasten the release of old negative karma.

But, few people appear to be aware of another more subtle "virus" that is extremely infectious. It is the "I want an interview" virus. I have observed that even with the very best intentions to resist this mental disease, it is extremely insidious and creeps in unawares despite every effort to avoid catching it, for it races through the crowds like wildfire. It acts in a way similar to mass hypnosis (hysteria) and is equally as powerful in its effect, for it renders its victims helpless to resist its overpowering influence. My own estimate is that about two weeks is the absolute limit for most people to remain unaffected by its grip. With people pleading, cajoling, demanding, and expecting an interview, it is extremely difficult to remain centered and remember that Baba himself is the only one who really knows who needs to be seen and who doesn't.

Many people mistakenly think that having an interview makes them special. They reason thus, "If God spoke to me I must be OK." So an interview is like a badge of approval. But Baba says that no one is special. None are better or worse. All are equal in his eyes.

My own experience leads me to believe that he appears to have at least three reasons for conferring this hoped-for boon:

1. The person is in great need of Baba's energy, encouragement, healing, or other type of help. So if Baba does not see someone it could mean that the particular individual is capable of handling his or her life and any problems he or she is facing and does not need Baba's special help. The inner Baba is sufficient.

2. The person comes in contact with a great number of people in his or her daily life and is therefore in a position to spread Baba's message to many others. Doctors, teachers, and all those who meet the public are in this category.

3. Baba knows he can use a particular person in some specific capacity to further his mission and is able to see the potential of that individual and his or her willingness to be guided and directed toward that end.

Most people want something from Baba and expect him to wave a magic wand to cure some physical illness, make them financially successful by providing them with a job they enjoy doing, bring into their life the perfect mate and ensure that they will bear perfect children, bless whatever other projects or wishes they bring to him to fulfill, give them precise instructions as well as his sanction of their pet schemes.

But Baba has said, "Avatars seldom give advice directly. Whatever they wish to communicate they convey more often by way of indirect suggestions and only rarely by the direct method of instruction. The reason for this is that there is divinity inherent in every human being, which he can manifest spontaneously, if favorable conditions are provided, just as viable seed will germinate and grow into a tree because of its inherent nature, if openly suitable facilities are provided for the manifestation of its potentiality. Man should be enabled to correct himself by his own efforts, by merely giving timely suggestions, rather than by stultifying his freedom and dignity through directives imposed from without. In short, the best maxim for helping people, either in worldly matters or in the spiritual field, is, 'Help them to help themselves,' or, 'Self-help is the best help.' ''

Sometimes someone will want Baba only to approve and bless his or her pet scheme or current plan. When Baba senses such a predetermination, he will often say, ''Yes, yes,'' as if he approves of it, knowing that the person's mind is so set on a specific outcome that he or she will pursue it anyway, whatever Baba's reaction might be. Unfortunately, many people take this to mean that Baba is giving his approval and will quote him by saying, ''Baba told me to do this or that,'' or, ''He said 'Yes' and gave his blessing.'' But it is always a good idea to observe the actual sequence of events and ask, ''Did Baba initiate the conversation or were his words in response to a preconceived plan being presented to him for his approval?''

Unless it is reined in, our monkey mind will try to grab what it wants, whether that happens to be a blessing on a plan of action, an assurance that we are making the right decision, or the desire to be approved of by Baba. But we tend to forget that he will rarely comment on such areas of our lives. His chief concern is our spiritual progress. Baba's mission, as he repeatedly reminds us, is to teach us who we really are and not merely to encourage our ego-determined actions, desires, and plans.

The word *darshan* means to see an evolved being and receive the energy transmitted by him. However, many people seem to be more interested in being seen by Baba, and to this end will do everything they can think of to attract his attention to them. Actually, he does see them but not always in a way that is apparent. His glance sweeps over all the eager faces turned up toward him, and he is immediately aware of those who need more personal attention to bolster their wavering faith, such as a look, a smile, or a word. But his actions are designed to strengthen their awareness and belief in their own inner Self and to encourage them to defer to It regularly for the help and guidance they need. In this way, he strives to wean us away from our dependence on his form as well as all other outer forms. When we are pleading for his attention, or even demanding it, our whole being is outwardly oriented in an assertive and sometimes even aggressive way. But Baba tells us that we need to be receptive in order to receive whatever he has to give us. So, if we are always trying to control the situation we are not open to receive from him.

In our breathing we alternate between inhaling and exhaling. Likewise, with prayer we need to ask, but we must also be sure to follow our requests by being open to receive the answer. Baba says that both men and women need to be feminine and receptive to his masculine or penetrating energy. So, in *darshan*, if we can breathe in his energy while he is visibly walking among us, we will receive far more from him than if we are constantly demanding what we want, but never relaxing sufficiently to be open to receive. If we breathe in his love and breathe out all our problems—as he has so often told us to do—we will be in a position to breathe in what he says he has come specifically to give us; namely, love. By this simple means, we can allow him to bring about profound changes within us that are necessary prerequisites for our eventual surrender to our own Higher Self. "Surrender, trust, and accept," is the motto for spiritual success.

PART II

HOW TO TAME
OUR MONKEY MIND

Chapter 16

Practical Spirituality

So far the spotlight has been turned on the monkey mind and all its many and varied antics. But, as we gain mastery over it and stop it from controlling our lives, we need to be provided with clear and simple steps to enable us to remain free from its control.

Life in this world is changing so much faster and more drastically in every area than ever before in recorded history, that we need new guidelines specifically designed for the present time. The old ones are no longer capable of helping with the present-day problems, since they were originally formulated with very different situations in mind.

The rapidly expanding drug scene, though very negative in its overall effect upon society, has one positive influence. It is such a widespread problem, and is affecting so many of the young people who will eventually be active in various aspects of their country's progress, that parents and other concerned adults are forced to recognize the crisis already upon us and address the need to find workable solutions.

As we look around us, read newspapers and magazines, watch television programs, listen to the news over the radio, read books, and attend current plays, we are made horribly aware of the extent of the problems facing not only this nation but the entire world. We are no longer allowed to concentrate solely on our own problems, for we are being bombarded with global ones so vast and complex in comparison that we instinctively turn away from having to absorb so much information, let alone try to discover possible solutions.

It is obvious to the majority of the inhabitants of this planet that the whole world faces more and more serious issues, which daunt the spirit of even the most brave and optimistic among us. But because these problems are all interconnected, we are unable to separate them into manageable parts that we might more easily handle. They are all so inextricably intertwined that we fail to see our way clear to attempt to solve even a small fraction of them.

Because so many changes have taken place so quickly and are so disturbing in their overall effect on people, there has not been enough time to formulate new guidelines more fitting to contemporary life. We are in urgent need of an itinerary, a blueprint, or a map to indicate the steps we must all be willing to take to lead us out of the world dilemma that has come upon us so suddenly. This is where Baba's teachings are so valuable *if* we apply them, for they point the way in such a simple fashion that even children can follow them. According to Baba, this is precisely why he incarnated at this particular time in history, as other avatars and world teachers have done at crucial times in the past. Baba says he has come to teach Practical Spirituality, which will help us answer his often-asked question, "Who are you?" which, in the past, other teachers have also asked their students.

He assures us that our true nature is an aspect of the Universal God-force that enlivens all living things. He also says that we are here on Earth to learn to accept this fact so that we can detach ourselves from our present personalities and the unreal security symbols we have been taught to revere, and begin to live as the gods we actually are at the core of our being.

So, Practical Spirituality means putting into practice in our own lives the various teachings that Baba has given us. For unless they are lived out each day they will have no real meaning for us nor will they bring about the required changes in our behavior. We need to espouse Practical Spirituality instead of merely having an intellectual interest in it if we ever hope to make our lives examples of Baba's message, as he says his is. Only when we are able to do so will we, like Hanuman, be servants of Rama, the personification of our own Reality. Then we can allow that wise and loving part to express Itself through the outer shell composed of the body, mind, ego and personality, and all the other layers we have gathered around us during our many sojourns in this world as human beings seeking our identity.

All the programs Baba has presented to us, as well as the many apt sayings he so patiently repeats and the many delightful teaching stories he relates, are designed to wake us up to the knowledge of who we really are so that we will allow him and his teachings to be lived out in our lives. In this way, others may also learn how to achieve freedom from the slavery of the senses that bind us to our physical forms.

Two old sayings I remember hearing countless times during my childhood come to mind: "Actions speak louder than words," and, "Practice what you preach." So many of us fail to bring into action the things we have learned. They remain in our heads where they do nothing to help us proceed toward our eventual goal of union with our real Self. It is useless merely to think about Baba's words and teachings. We can all do that and still remain exactly the same with no change in our behavior. It is equally useless only to speak about them, read them, or listen to them. For Baba's teachings to become part of our lives we must put them into operation. Only then will they bear fruit for us. So, instead of talking about being spiritual, let us all concentrate on *being* spiritual and practicing what we preach, which is the only way we are ever likely to encourage others to do the same. For we cannot practice for anyone else any more than someone else can for us. To think otherwise is an escape from our immediate task, which is to work on ourselves and leave others to do the same, if and when they wish to.

But we all have the gift of free will or free choice, so we need to make a commitment to bring every detail of our lives in line with Baba's message and allow our petty little egos and wills to be yoked (as in yoga) to his will so that we really mean it when we say, "Thy will, not mine, be done." Baba tells us we are all walking temples, so it behooves each of us to act as if that were so by cleaning our temple to make it a fit place for the God we really are to inhabit.

It takes only a very small amount of yeast to raise a large lump of dough in the baking of bread. In the same way, a mere handful of dedicated individuals could have a similar effect on the current global situation. By raising our own consciousness, the state of the world could automatically be lifted to a higher level, which in turn would benefit everyone if they were open to growth. To many people such an idea will seem like a pipe dream. However, the overall situation in every country of the world is so dark and frightening—and worsening more and more every day—that we have nothing to lose by trying. Only a few willing workers are needed to bring about a change, and what a wonderful challenge that can be for all those who are becoming aware of the disturbing signs of decay all around them.

But in order to be among the pioneers of this new way of life, we must first put our own lives in order. One of the easiest and most practical ways to achieve that is by practicing the simple and clear steps Baba so patiently continues to outline, not only for his so-called devotees, but for anyone in the whole world who is ready to listen.

Chapter 17

Putting Spirituality into Daily Practice

As I have already mentioned, we are to a large extent unconscious of our habits, behavior, attitudes, and insecurities. The roles we play and the masks we hide behind are used to avoid honestly facing ourselves and all our deficiencies. But many people do not fully realize that to be unconscious of something means literally to have absolutely no knowledge or perception of it. It is as if we are blind and cannot see ourselves at all clearly. That is the reason it is so much easier to catch glimpses of our own traits in other people and their actions or in the characters that appear in our dreams.

Another way in which we can start to observe the effect we have on other people is to make a determined effort to be more aware, by watching the effects of our words, behavior, expressions, and general attitude on all those with whom we come into contact. The best way to detect how they react to us is to look at their eyes and observe their body language. Do they wince, or turn away, or drop their eyes when we use a particular tone of voice? Do they appear to shrink into themselves when we deliver a lecture that is often an attempt on our part to build up our own self-esteem and confidence, but at another's expense? Are we condescending in our attitude or tone of voice when addressing those who serve us in some capacity, such as waiters and waitresses, salespeople, those who work at the check-out stands in markets, garage attendants who refuel our cars, housekeepers, hairdressers, and a host of other public servants? At such times it is helpful to remember that Baba has told us that we are all equal in his eyes, as he sees only the Atma, our real Self.

We must also watch our attitude toward those whom we consider to be important in some way. Are we obsequious? Do we rush to agree with them even when we really do not approve of what they say or how they act? Do we curry favor with those we think might be useful to us and ignore those who are not in a position to do us a favor?

We are all suffering from some type of insecurity, due to the fact that we have been taught to rely on tangible objects and other people for security instead of our own real Self. We all express our particular insecurity in many different ways, one of the most obvious ones being a tendency to boast in a mistaken attempt to build up our importance, often at the expense of others. But whatever we do to others we are, in fact, doing to ourselves, since we are all one at the Source. At some future time, when the circumstances warrant it, we will find ourselves placed in a situation in which we are on the receiving end of whatever we have done to others in the past, both the kind acts and words and the harsh or demeaning ones.

So in the end, it behooves us to practice what Baba teaches by monitoring our thoughts, feelings, words, and actions in our daily dealings with those with whom we come in contact. As we do so, we may be dismayed at the negative tone of our behavior. We can then ask Baba to help us by thinking, feeling, speaking, and acting through us—with love!

Chapter 18

Practical Spirituality in the Home

Thus far we have considered behavior toward members of the general public. However, the way we speak and behave around members of our own family also needs to be scrutinized. We can be polite, tolerant, and compassionate to those we meet outside the home, but wreak our anger, hostility, and resentment on our immediate family members. This is one of the most common causes of the increasing number of cases of battered spouses and children.

It is a well-known fact that many of those charged with assault and battery are often described by their associates as being very pleasant and considerate individuals. That may be true in their dealings with others. However, many times they do not really want to be so obliging, but for some reason they are afraid not to be. So they resort to suppressing their resentment, anger, and frustration for the time being, only to unleash it on to their spouse and children at the slightest provocation. They are on their best behavior with strangers and acquaintances but let out all their frustrations at home.

Practical spirituality should start in the home. We can check our own record by asking ourselves some pertinent questions: Are we as polite to our husband or wife as we are to our boss or coworkers? Do we watch the effect of our tone of voice on our children? Do we ever praise them or give them credit where it is due, or do we resort to constant criticism, sarcasm, and petty fault-finding? Do we remember to express our feelings of love and affection, or do we expect those with whom we share our home to be able to read our minds in order to find out how we feel about them?

Baba tells us that everything we do all day, every day should be worship, that we should not label certain activities more spiritual than others and leave other people to engage in the latter for us while we selfishly do only those things we consider to be more spiritual.

Baba has given us many different exercises to develop discipline, such as meditation, *japamala*, *bhajan* singing, and so forth, but he warns that none of these is capable of taking us any closer to enlightenment. In this dark age called *Kali Yuga* (in Sanskrit), only *seva* (or service) to humanity can further our spiritual growth, and service should start at home with family members, as they are the very ones who can teach us the most and whom we can teach by our example more than by our words.

I am your raft on the ocean deep,
I am the eye of the storm.
I am the wind which will blow you clean,
I am you before you were born.

Cling to me as I am,
Question but do not doubt.
Trust my truth with all your might
Through storm or war or drought.

Rise to your toes and hold on to me.
Do not grovel on the ground.
Reach for the sun which is my power
And listen for my sound.

Hold on tight and never let go.
I am me but I'm also you.
Stretch to your utmost as you go
Forward to meet me-you.

Chapter 19

You Cannot Always Oblige, but You Should Always Speak and Act Obligingly

In addition to the above advice from Baba, he also advises us thus: "When someone insults you or defames you or ignores you, accept it with a smile. This is the way of the world. It is basically ill-mannered. Say to yourself, 'They are doing me a good turn, my strength is under trial. I should not yield to anger or resentment.' When you do not accept the insult someone casts on you, it goes back to the person who sent it. A registered letter that is not accepted returns to the sender. So do not damage your mutual peace by receiving the letter and reading its contents. Refuse to receive it."

In his daily schedule, Baba sets us all a wonderful example by putting this teaching into practice. During just one day he is in contact with the many thousands who eagerly flock to him from all parts of the world to receive his blessing, to be re-energized, and to be reminded of who they really are. In addition, he meets an untold number of individuals and groups on a more direct and personal basis, either in quick encounters during *darshan* or in group and personal interviews.

This routine is repeated every day, all year long, and has been happening for over fifty years. Yet, with all the diverse ways in which people react to him, he floats through the hours unruffled, his serenity unaffected whatever their behavior. Some people are worshipful, some anxious. Some are hopeful for a boon and others doubtful and depressed. Some are shy while others are pushy, some are happy, and many are sad. A veritable barrage of varied emotions greet him wherever he goes each day. It would be far too much for any of us to face, yet he appears to be unaffected. He ignores some and smiles at others, speaks to one or two and gently waves back those who try to crash through the lines to hand him a letter or to touch his feet. Even when he sees the need to restrain someone's unruly behavior, he does it with firmness laced with his ceaseless flow of love and compassion.

No, he does not always oblige by any means, but he speaks and acts obligingly and directs us to mold our words and actions on the example he sets us. However, it is not at all easy to follow his example. We speak and act so often without first stopping to consider the effect our words and deeds may have on the recipients. Many of us are apt to control our speech and actions with people we admire and whose approval we seek, or those we hold in awe, or anyone of whom we are afraid. In addition, there is the temptation to be obliging to people who are in a position to do us a favor, or when we know we are being observed, which are both selfish reasons. In other words, we are obliging only when it suits us to be. But what about our words and actions when there is no audience to admire us, or when we are interacting with people we consider to be inferior or unimportant, or when we encounter those we do not like? And what about the members of our family?

There is also another frequent though quite different reaction. There are those who feel they have to do whatever anyone asks or expects them to do. They oblige or conform to someone else's demands, even though they are fully aware that to do so would be in opposition to what they believe to be right. This is not what Baba means. He says, "You may not always be able to oblige," so there are times when to do so would not be right. At such times we need to be strong enough and have sufficient courage to resist the pressure or persuasion of anyone who tries to control us to act at variance to our own principles. This question is particularly applicable to children and young people who meet with peer pressure to indulge in drugs, alcohol, sex, or any other activity that their peers want to force them to participate in against their better judgment.

The emphasis is solely on our attitude. Can we say "No" in such a way that we avoid the trap of demeaning ourselves by groveling or apologizing out of all proportion to the situation? And can we hold firmly to our own convictions of what is correct, yet do so in a way that we are not offensive and do not put others on the defense? It is not an easy assignment. But little by little, as we become more firmly and habitually aware of our true identity, we will be able to lubricate our words and deeds with love, as Baba does. That will automatically soften our speech and actions so that they are obliging and pleasant despite our refusal always to oblige.

I have been fascinated to observe that when I am being coerced into doing something I do not want to do—yet lack a strong feeling of security in my own decision—I become nervous, anxious, and even angry. Then these emotions color my words and actions and stir up negative reactions in the other person. However, if I stay calm and firm in my resolve with no emotional overlay, to my surprise and delight the person will invariably accept my refusal quite calmly and without the usual emotional eruption. If in addition, I can try to visualize the God-self within the personality and behind the assumed mask of control, and can breathe love to that facsimile of my own God-self, the person will often melt like a little kitten. Baba reminds us that, "Love is the solvent for the hardest of hearts." We know this to be true, but we all forget to practice it.

Chapter 20

Be Here Now

Baba says, "The past is beyond recovery. The future is uncertain. The given moment is now." He also points out that it is usually older people who hark back to the past and mourn the passing of the "good old days" and the young people whose gaze is so often fixed on the future. But he assures us neither is practical, for only in the present can we forge our future.

Many people spend a large part of their lives escaping from the present. This escape takes many different forms, but whatever method is involved, it allows the monkey mind to be in control. That means that the individual wastes the opportunity this present life makes possible to learn some things that were never learned before. As soon as we give up control of our lives to the monkey mind, it takes over and we become its victim.

Admittedly, life at the present time can often be labeled dull and boring, tedious and monotonous, dreary and depressing, grim and painful, and a whole host of other such apt descriptions. But, we ourselves are responsible for these attitudes toward our lives. It is not, as we often prefer to think, life itself and the attendant circumstances, experiences, and events that are in control. We all have a measure of free will that we can use to the best advantage by changing our own attitude. The old example of "seeing life through rose-colored spectacles" still has merit, but only when interpreted correctly. It does not mean that we should behave insincerely like a Pollyanna, pretending that our life is a bed of roses and everything is perfect.

But our approach to life can lead us to examine aspects we find difficult and help us find a way of dispensing with them, or mitigating them, or changing them in such a way that they become assets instead of liabilities. In addition, we can ask ourselves what they can teach us. Could it be patience, which almost everyone is lacking? Might it be tolerance or a "live-and-let-live" attitude? Or, more importantly, could people be used as a mirror in which to catch a glimpse of our own problems or weaknesses that our present life is designed to help us erase? All of these, and many other points, can help change our attitude about whatever we are facing, whether it is a difficult relationship, ill health, lack of a job or adequate means with which to support ourselves and our families, or dozens of other so-called problems.

Problems need to be solved. If life is compared to a school our circumstances are our assignments, and they will prove to be the very means to help us progress from where we are in the school of life to the next grade up the scale. We have all experienced the thrill and sense of fulfillment that comes from finally tackling a particularly unpleasant task that we have been studiously avoiding. The same pleasing sense of accomplishment accompanies every effort we make to stop ourselves from escaping and begin to view demanding situations as potential blessings in disguise. That alone will help us strengthen our spiritual muscles.

And what are these escape hatches through which we disappear, mistakenly believing that we are free from the responsibilities we are trying to avoid? Many addictions can offer us an escape from the present, particularly the use of any hallucinogenic drugs. The time they consume is lost forever and we are no nearer our essential goal. There are other less tangible avenues of escape, which can be even more seductive, such as daydreams, fantasies, and wishful thinking in which we all indulge from time to time. When they become a habit, however, and consume too much of our lives, they can be likened to thieves. It is natural to have hopes, aspirations, and dreams. It is only when they take up so much time and energy that we are left with too little of either to use for tasks at hand that they become escapes from daily living. In addition, if they remain airborne and are never brought into manifestation, which is often the case, they are even more of a menace to our well-being.

On a much grander scale than our personal fantasies, and therefore far more powerful, are those concocted by some authors. Even more powerful are the creations of movie and television writers. These flickering images seductively invade our living rooms and lure us into vicariously living the glamorous roles portrayed on the screen instead of our own more mundane lives.

All these decoys take our attention away from our own particular path with its various challenges and lessons to be learned. In effect they cheat us out of our birthright, our only legitimate escape from the wheel of life and death, which is actually not an escape but a graduation, for it has to be earned. We can only learn from our own set of circumstances and not from anyone else's—definitely not from fictitious characters and their imaginary lives.

The antidote to these escape tactics is to "practice the presence" as the early Christian writers expressed it. Since Baba teaches that the Presence is our real Self within our outer physical form, we can dedicate all we do to It and ask that It live through us and guide us on our way. Then we can achieve "presence of mind" and will also increasingly "be here now."

So, besides my usual morning ritual of asking Baba to think, feel, speak, act, and love through me all day, I put the reins into his hands, so to speak, and talk to him at intervals during the day. For instance, when I am driving on the highway with cars hurtling past on either side and crowding or tailgating behind, I give the whole scene over to Baba. I ask him to be the driver instead of my personal self, and to keep the other cars at a safe distance. It is quite startling to watch the scene through my rearview mirror— a car too close for comfort looks as if it might plow into me at any minute. I see it slow down and gradually leave more space between us and, surprisingly enough, the car remains at that distance from then on. I often wonder what the driver must be thinking about the way he reacts.

I continue this same inner dialogue whatever I am doing—that is, if I remember! I ask him to indicate which letters I should answer, and to write through me as I pen each reply. When I am working with someone who has problems, using the counseling method I have learned, I ask him to tell me what to do or say or what exercises to suggest "to help them help themselves," which Baba says is so much better than to do it for them. It is often most surprising to have an idea enter my mind, which I am absolutely certain I personally did not originate, that proves to be exactly what the person needs at that time.

We all need to practice being here now. In order to learn how to do this, we need to constantly pull the monkey mind back from its wanderings into the past or into the future. It also means that we need to watch out for wishful thinking, escaping into imaginary situations, or all those other places the monkey mind can lure us into. When we are successful at dealing with the monkey mind, we will be able to get our work done in less time; we will find that we have plenty of time and energy to spend on more creative things—or more fun things.

My heart leaps up when I behold
Your vibrant red-clad form
As you emerge into our view
To quell the gathering storm.

The world is in deep trouble,
No one knew quite what to do
Until you came to tell us
That the cure resides in you.

We have heard that many teachers
Have come at times like this
To show mankind how to achieve
A state of permanent bliss.

This time you come to teach us
Not to run away from life
But to seek God's strength within us
In the midst of all the strife.

You say we're not our bodies
But that deep within we'll find
A god-like aspect of ourselves
That's wise and strong and kind.

And if we will remember,
As we start afresh each day,
Quite silently beneath our breath
A mantra we can say.

That will help us to be calmer
And we'll find that we can cope
As we turn our backs on worry
And replace our fears with hope.

What is this magic mantra
That such miracles can achieve?
"I am God and not the body.
This I verily do believe!"

Chapter 21

Getting Control of the Monkey Mind

Monkeys are renowned both for their love of food and their fascination with brightly colored or glittering objects. They have no hesitation in stealing any such baubles they spy that are left within their reach. Many times when we have been in India in places where many monkeys congregate, either we ourselves or others have been victims of their rapacity. We have learned from such experiences never to leave fruit or nuts near an open window through which they can enter the room, devour them in minutes, and dash off to find more plunder, leaving behind a veritable mess of discarded rinds, shells, pits, and sticky juice.

The same caution has to be applied regarding jewelry or any brightly colored or sparkling trinkets that might attract their roving eye if left unattended within their sight and reach. For they will not hesitate to snatch and carry off such booty far from the owner's reach, making it impossible to retrieve.

If we are stringently honest we will have to admit that many human beings, perhaps ourselves included, have retained similar tendencies inherited from our evolution from the animal kingdom. But, we do not need to remain at this primitive stage of consciousness. We have the choice of taking the evolutionary steps from animal to human and from human to divine with enlightenment or "at-onement" with the High Self as the eventual goal. However, to achieve this goal, it is essential to gain control over the monkey mind that anchors us to the body and its myriad desires, and prevents us from taking even one step toward our real identity.

Baba describes the function of the physical form thus: "The body with all its equipment of senses, intellect, feeling, and memory is an instrument, an implement, a chariot one uses for movement toward a goal. The owner of the chariot is on any day more important than the chariot itself; it is for his sake that it has to be kept trim and efficient and in good repair. The duration of life is under the control of Him who gave life, the Creator."

So, how can we gain control over the wayward mind that is so easily enticed away from the goal by everything that attracts its attention through the five senses? When we have become aware of how it dashes hither and yon to grab hold of whatever it can see, hear, smell, taste, or feel, how can we restrain it? Like the monkey with its fist trapped in the bottle, we think we too are trapped and incapable of setting ourselves free. But that is not the case at all. As soon as the mind relinquishes whatever is holding it captive, it can assume control over the senses instead of allowing them to dominate it. Then the mind can be used for its rightful purpose: to discover what needs to be done before the next step can be taken to become fully human.

But to ensure success in this endeavor it is absolutely essential to request help and guidance from the High Self, symbolized by Rama, and to obey Its slightest command as Hanuman learned to do. To quote Baba again, "Hanuman obeyed Rama implicitly without question and succeeded. He did not calculate the danger engendered by a course of action and hesitate; he did not feel proud that he was chosen for the task and enthuse. He listened, he understood; he obeyed and he won. The name Ramadutha, Messenger, servant of Rama that he earned thereby made him immortal. You must earn the name Sai Rama Dutha. Have fortitude and self-control; use good and sweet words; examine each act of yours on the touchstone of my preference; will Swami approve of it? It is a lifelong task and you must continue the discipline and be bright lamps to light the path for others." Only in this way can we be free from the self-inflicted fetters with which our senses have enslaved our minds and, in turn, have rendered us helpless to free ourselves.

By regularly turning within and asking for help and then listening for direction, we will be able gradually to withdraw from the overwhelming thrall of *Maya*, or illusion, and be free to allow our real Self to express Itself through us until It takes over completely and we become one with Its light, which is the meaning of enlightenment.

In the reverie work with which I have been occupied for many years, I have been shown various methods that help to control the monkey mind. One of them consists of actually visualizing the mind as a monkey. I usually recall the little monkey I saw at the wharf in Monterey accompanying its master the organ-grinder. This tiny, almost human-looking animal was dressed in a miniature jacket, baggy pants, full-sleeved shirt, bright red waistcoat, and, to complete the outfit, a fez secured by a strap under its chin. It also wore a harness to which was attached a leash that allowed its master to pull it back whenever its curiosity took it too far afield for him to coax it to perform for the crowd. This restraint is exactly what we all need to use with our own monkey mind to stop it from straying too far and attaching us to whatever it sees, hears, smells, tastes, or touches that appeals to it.

Another useful method for controlling the monkey mind is reminiscent of deep-sea fishing. Those who set out to catch marlin or other large fighting fish are strapped into a harness attached to the fishing boat. It firmly supports and steadies them when the fish they have on their line resists being captured and swims off as fast as possible to try to escape from being reeled in. Using this image to reel in the monkey mind, we can visualize its eyes darting this way and that in search of some appealing object. The mind can be deliberately pulled back exactly as a fish is reeled in on a line. In this way we will gradually regain control of the monkey mind, which can then lead quite naturally to control of the senses. The final result will allow us to take our rightful role as master—with the senses returning to their role of very useful servants—instead of allowing the senses to assume the role of very unreliable masters and reducing us to acting as their servant.

Another method to control the monkey mind is to imagine riding a horse that is attracted by something it wants to investigate off the path we wish to follow. If this were actually the case, we would press our feet firmly in the stirrups and rein in the horse, using everything we had ever learned in riding school to bring the horse under our control instead of allowing it to take us where it wants to go. The mind can be reined in and controlled in a similar way.

Another very simple little exercise that is very helpful in containing the mind I call the "Tape Measure," which is an apt description of the mind with its habit of measuring everything with which it comes into contact. To contain the mind and bring it under our control, we visualize it as a retractable tape measure neatly coiled in a case. We imagine pulling it out against its spring to the furthest extent. This represents the mind being allowed to have full play. Then, it needs to be released and snapped back into the case and placed firmly to one side to restrain its undisciplined activity. It has proved to be even more helpful to purchase a retractable tape measure to have on hand as a reminder, as well as to make the exercise more realistic and therefore more potent in its effect.

Some people may object to such simple devices, dubbing them childish and forgetting that the simpler and more pictorial the directions, the easier it is to put them into practice. Children have much to teach adults by their quick acceptance of visualization exercises. They have had less time than adults to accumulate habits and patterns of thinking that prevent new ideas from being accepted. This is undoubtedly what is meant by, "Except ye be converted, and become as little children, ye shall not enter into the kingdom of heaven" (Matthew 18:3). We all need to be childlike—but not childish—and to be guided only by the High Self, which will give us entry into the kingdom of heaven within each of us.

Chapter 22

Fact or Fiction—
Inspired Knowledge or Thought

Some thoughts contain grains of truth interwoven with fiction, which actually makes it even easier to believe they are true and reliable, though harder to differentiate between truth and fiction. According to Baba, "Thoughts originate in the mind, they express themselves through words, and are materialized through deeds," which would indicate that thinking is a private, individual, or personal activity. We continuously create with our minds thoughts, and the multiple thought-forms they produce, all day long every day. But, what we fail to realize is that these thoughts are our own creations, stemming from our limited personal experience, background, early conditioning, and current situation. They are, therefore, not necessarily true or even factual. Also, since they are our own purely personal creation, and merely express our version of truth or reality, they are not always applicable or meaningful to other people, even though we may try to force-feed them to others as if they represented the indisputable truth for everyone.

So, each of us lives with this monkey mind of ours chattering away all day long about everything under the sun, busily spinning a web composed of both fact and fiction. Unfortunately, like those parents who believe their children can do no wrong, we too often tend to feel the same way about these "brain children" we create with our thoughts, which, though they have no real substance, can exert tremendous control over their creator. We often hear people say that certain thoughts continuously race around in their mind like a squirrel in a cage. Most of us, at some time in our lives, have helplessly experienced the control such obsessive thoughts wield over us, but have known of no way to put a stop to it.

Thinking is a human function that includes reasoning, imagining, inventing, calculating, fantasizing, and various other ways in which we use the mind. But it is only one of four functions at our disposal; the other three are sensation, feeling, and intuition, all equally useful tools. Thinking also happens to be the one most recently developed during the evolutionary process in human beings. Therefore, it has assumed undue importance in many people's estimation; so much so that the other functions have been neglected in its favor, which has resulted in the intellect and the ability to think being more highly revered, sometimes almost to the point of worship.

But there is a vast difference between what we think and the wisdom or knowledge of Truth that is available to us when we are willing to receive it from our High Self and calm the busy mind and listen to Its inner voice. We think we know what is good for us as well as what would have the opposite effect, but as our thoughts are not to be trusted since we ourselves have created them, not only are they not necessarily true, but they are also capable of unexpected changes. We have all experienced thinking that something is good or desirable and then, after being given more facts about it, changed our minds and started thinking exactly the opposite. So thought is obviously not always a reliable indicator of what is correct or incorrect. It merely presents us with a view of our personal preferences and aversions according to the way our senses have lured our monkey mind into becoming attached to certain objects, ideas, opinions, beliefs, superstitions, and the vast mass of human thought.

Because thoughts are not always based on truth but on our own concoctions—often containing other people's thoughts, our own fantasies, misconceptions, fears, and many other ingredients of this mental brew—they are unreliable guides to lead us to live more happily, fully, and productively. But if the mind—on which we have been taught to rely for guidance—cannot be trusted, what or who can we trust to show us what to do and what not to do so that we can begin to live more successfully?

The intellect or the process of thinking is part of the fallible body-mind-ego-personality sheath or outer covering over the real Self. It is a tool together with the other tools we have been given; all excellent if used properly and harmoniously together, and even more so when directed by the High Self instead of by the monkey mind. But we have been educated in such a way that we continue to believe that what we think is the absolute truth until proved otherwise. This often causes even more lack of confidence in ourselves and our ability to live successfully. So how can we tell the difference between a thought that can be fictitious and truth or inspired knowledge, and therefore between our own thoughts and the inner direction from the High Self?

Inspired knowledge or wisdom has come down through the ages in many different forms according to the person or group of people through whom it was transmitted. All the original doctrines of the various religions were based on received or inspired truth rather than intellectualized concepts. This wisdom was vital and immediate and perfectly adapted to the people to whom it was given at that time. It had not yet had time to become congealed into specific belief systems as we know them by being overlaid with many people's thoughts. It sprang from direct personal reception of Truth instead of being borrowed from other people's experience.

Such knowledge is like a river flowing uncontaminated directly from the pure Source into the mind of the recipient. All the ancient writings and the verbal teachings of all the nations in the world originally contained this true pure knowledge. But as the priests and elders changed or deleted various parts of it to enable them to control the people with their own fallacious ideas, the original truth became diluted and in some cases even destroyed or lost. However, much of it has been preserved, hidden in myths, fairy tales, rituals, mystery plays, legends, songs, nursery rhymes and children's games, and even in playing cards such as the tarot deck. This ancient wisdom had to be sent underground to save it from being extinguished by those who were powerful enough to destroy it in order to impose their own control over the masses. It was often transmitted in symbols that needed to be deciphered to reveal the messages they contained, and was carried safely and un-recognized until those with sufficient insight were able to understand and use it.

Baba frequently quotes at length from the Indian ex-positions of this original Truth contained in the Vedas, the Bhagavad Gita, the Mahabharatha, and other writings. He urges us to study these teachings and glean from them the inspired wisdom they contain to counteract the pro-liferation of fake belief systems circulating in the world today. This source of true knowledge can also be directly contacted when we slow our thinking and consciously seek guidance from the High Self, which automatically by-passes the control of our conscious mind as well as the negative or fallacious thought-forms composed of the countless thoughts of individuals over many centuries.

Baba has also given us five stepping-stones to help us discriminate between our own thoughts and the direction we can receive from the High Self when we admit that we do not know and ask It for help. They can also be used as a yardstick to measure our progress when we regularly check our behavior against them. They are *sathya, dharma, shanti, prema,* and *ahimsa.*

Sathya means Truth. We need to determine how we would rate ourselves against this value, but we have to be brutally honest as we do so. Have we been totally honest today in our dealings with others? If not, what were the occasions when we deviated from the truth? What were our reasons for doing so? Being honest with ourselves also comes under this heading. Do we pretend to be perfect in comparison with others? Do we report an event or describe a situation accurately, or do we tend to exaggerate and embroider it to make it appear more amusing or interesting to ourselves and others? These are just a few suggested ways to check our own honesty. We can also observe the message we are receiving to determine whether it issues from the pure Source or from our own ego by asking ourselves if it rings true or feels false. But many people are still unsure about the messages and need more definite reassurance of their authenticity. I can recall the time when I asked to be given a specific sign to reassure me, and to my surprise I immediately experienced what reminded me of a cold shower flowing down my spine. Other people who have asked for a sign have reported that they have felt a tingling in the middle of their forehead, pins and needles in some part of their body, or a tingling sensation in their palms or the soles of their feet, and many other similar manifestations. So the best way is to ask for a sign that will indicate that the message issues from the real Self and not from the ego or personal desire.

Dharma is usually translated as right action. However, it means more than that. It is the action or behavior that is appropriate or fitting for the different situations we may face in life. The *dharmic* way to act or live for one person in this station in life would not necessarily be the same for someone else with a different set of circumstances. We can also check the input we receive when consulting the High Self against this yardstick to see how it fits.

Shanti means peace, but Baba says, "*Shanti* is not merely peace. It is something which transcends peace. It is the calm of the mind, serenity of the mind that makes you find inner peace and total stability within yourself. *Shanti* plays a great role in any integrated personality's life and conduct." Again, "*shanti* or peace is the most priceless possession of man. It is the sign of a virtuous character, a willingness to serve, a readiness to renounce, a calm spirit of resignation, an awareness of the evanescence of material wealth, and of the cool agitationless lake of joy in the heart."

Prema means love. Not the human kind that Baba calls "contraction love," which leads people to grasp, smother, and seek to possess others, but Baba's kind of love, "expansion love," which includes all living beings in its embrace. He says, "Love is reverence when directed toward parents, companionship when it flows toward friends, passion when it is felt toward the partner, respect when it moves toward elders, affection when you are drawn toward children, and devotion when directed toward God."

Ahimsa, Baba tells us, can best be described as "reverence for all life in thought, word, and deed."

He sums up the combination of all five thus:

> *Sathya is man's nature.*
> *Dharma is its practical application.*
> *Shanti or peace is the result of Dharma, and*
> *Prema is the effulgence of Shanti.*

He also says,

> *Where there is faith there is Love*
> *Where there is Love there is Peace*
> *Where there is Peace there is Truth*
> *Where there is Truth there is God*

Each one of us is capable of dipping into the vast reservoir of knowledge that is available to those who diligently search for Truth. Our direct contact is possible by way of the spark of Divinity within each and every living being. We can tune into It if we have true humility and admit that we do not have all the answers ourselves. We also have to be able to admit that with the ego alone we are not able to cope with life's challenges, opportunities, tragedies, losses, disappointments and frustrations, and all the other threads that make up the fabric of daily living. Then we can make contact with that aspect of the whole that we carry within us and of which we are all a part.

Chapter 23

The Spiritual Striptease

Before we can undertake to put Baba's teachings into daily practice, we will have to discard some of the habits of thinking that prevent us from even making a start in that direction. Since thought is necessary before any action can take place, we can catch sight of our thoughts by watching our behavior. Then we need to ask ourselves, "Where do our thoughts come from and how are they formed?"

It appears from observation that thoughts spring from several different sources. We bring many thought patterns with us from past lives. We absorb the thoughts of our parents, particularly those of the mother even while we are still in her womb. From birth through childhood, we draw from the energy fields formed by the thoughts of the various members of the family into which we were born; this provides us with the necessary lessons to be learned in our present life. Then later in life thoughts are supplied by the various teachers in the schools we attend, the books we read, the religious disciplines to which we are exposed, and the political affiliation of our parents. Eventually ideas are added that we ourselves espouse, as well as thoughts from many other sources throughout our lives, and we end up by carrying layer upon layer of false or borrowed beliefs. These prevent us from expressing or even uncovering our own truth, which lies hidden within us until we make a conscious effort to seek it by turning away from all the acquired knowledge and becoming receptive to the inspired wisdom that is then attainable. But before we can open up our minds to this true knowledge, we need to chip away the thick layers of acquired half-truths that have accumulated around us like barnacles that obscure from view who we really are. This involves a spiritual striptease.

In addition to this unhealthy and cluttered situation, there is another even more serious problem. Everything ever created in the world by human beings started as a thought in someone's mind. Thought is the builder of tangible objects, but also of everything manifested on all the other levels whether physical, mental, emotional, psychic, or spiritual. When we accept a certain concept as being based in truth, we automatically form a connection to the universal thought form that has been built up around it over many centuries, created from all the thoughts of countless individuals on that specific subject. It is easy to understand that these universal thought forms have become very, very powerful, since they have gathered more and more energy with each contributor's thoughts. When our own thoughts are on the same wavelength as the universal ones, a connection is automatically formed. But, as these universal thought-forms are so much more powerful than any individual, we come under their influence and end up being controlled by them and helpless to break free from their domination, even if we wish to. We are then enslaved by a force far greater than our own personal will. This condition provides one of the explanations for the strong hold certain addictions exert over people from which they frequently discover, to their dismay, they are unable to free themselves.

As we continue to be controlled by these powerful thought-forms, we are still continuously contributing to their power with our own thoughts, and are therefore also guilty of increasing their hold on others who—like ourselves—are also connected to them. It is a veritable vicious circle and one of which most people are completely unaware.

We as individuals are responsible for the effect of our thoughts, not only on ourselves and our own lives, but also on the whole world and everything and everyone inhabiting it and sharing it with us. But many people shy away from assuming any responsibility for their thoughts, preferring to blame conditions, other people, fate, and a host of other imagined causes for their plight, forgetting that whatever happens to an individual is not an accident. Each of us, during our present life and in past incarnations, has launched out into the universe an unlimited number of thoughts and the feelings that accompany them—some positive but many very often negative in content. However, our own personal strength will soon prove to be thoroughly inadequate to free us, for only with the help of the High Self, which is connected to limitless power, can we hope to break the connection and retrieve our birthright of free will.

Alcoholics Anonymous groups, among others, have successfully wrenched many individuals away from slavery to their addiction to alcohol by invoking the aid of a Higher Power. But it is not only substances such as liquor and drugs that enslave the user's mind. Any powerful thought form created by a strong belief held by many people can have a similar effect. Many times when I have sought guidance from the High Self the directions I have received have been in direct opposition to my own opinions, which were gleaned from many sources during my life. In this way, I have been instructed to correct erstwhile false beliefs and replace them with received knowledge that alone is valid for the particular situation at that precise time. This experience explains so well a fact that has caused much confusion regarding Baba. He has been known to give an answer to one person's question and offer an entirely different answer to the same question asked by a different person, or he even sometimes gives a different answer to the same question asked by the same person on another occasion.

Baba presents us with a perfect example of one who is always in touch with true knowledge and who knows how it fits the immediate situation as well as the attitude of each person at the exact moment when he or she is seeking an answer. If we are fully surrendered and open to receive the correct answer that is what we will be given, but if we still insist on our own desire or preference, we will be given a different answer. Baba will often say, "Yes, yes," not necessarily to indicate agreement, but simply because he realizes the individual will do what he or she wants anyway and is only seeking Baba's sanction.

Baba is here to teach us how to make contact with the totally reliable guidance available to those who are willing to detach themselves from all the old familiar belief systems borrowed from others, and, with patience and perseverance, seek it from within. He is able to bring forth this wisdom instantly because he exists in this living flow and has none of the multitudes of accretions to remove, as we have. But he urges us not to become so attached to his form that we insist on asking him personally the questions that can and should be answered by the source within us. Only by deferring to this inner source of wisdom can we become Self-confident, Self-dependent, and Self-motivated.

Baba explains that the ancient Vedic chants are composed of symbolic words filled with energy from the original Source whence they emerged. Chanting them or listening to others chanting them can put us in touch with this continuous flow of Truth if we detach ourselves from all the bodies of organized thought and discipline and are willing to tune in afresh to our own connection to this source of all knowledge. It reminds me of an assembly line carrying certain truths that become available at specific times. As an example, inventors, composers, and artists of all kinds have gained access to this flow of inspiration and have learned how to bring into manifestation a particular insight that is available at a certain time, only to discover later that other people had simultaneously made contact with the same truth. This phenomenon explains why an inventor in one part of the world produces an apparently new idea—believing it to be his alone—only to learn that several other people have "invented" or discovered the same thing, all completely unaware of the others' inventions. Apparently, they all made contact with whatever was being revealed at that time and proceeded to make it available to the world. For all insights have to be worked out on a personal and concrete level if they are to be useful.

So how are we to begin to listen within to the "still small voice" of the High Self? The Zen Buddhist Masters and other teachers throughout the world and down the centuries have given their pupils exercises to help them still the mind, or, as they often expressed it, to "create a space between two thoughts." The Zen teachers also gave a koan (or riddle) to distract the busy mind and give it something to occupy its attention by setting it to work on a riddle that had no rational solution and was therefore impossible to decipher. When the mind finally gave up its efforts in utter exhaustion and confusion, an insight or inspiration was able to enter, because it was no longer blocked by the melee of thoughts usually filling it.

There are many other methods for freeing the mind from incessant activity so that it is open to receive wisdom from the High Self. Baba offers a remedy to keep the mind concentrated and out of mischief. He suggests that we keep one of the many names that refer to God or the Universal Life-force always on the tongue. He explains that when the mind is engaged in so engrossing an activity it allows inspiration from the real Self to come through. In addition, this method encourages us to defer more and more to the real Source and turn away from false, fictitious, or faulty information.

This method reminds me of the little monkey and its master, the organ-grinder. When it was allowed to run and jump here and there, wherever its fancy carried it, it would get into all kinds of trouble. But when its master was holding it firmly by the leash and giving it orders to shake hands or perform other tricks, it was perfectly well behaved and orderly in its conduct. Being so similar in behavior to the monkey, our mind needs to be kept under control and engaged in productive pursuits so that it does not start to control us with its constant nonsensical chatter.

When someone asks me how to get in touch with the High Self, I always think of the way we change gears while driving a car. It is just as simple to move the mind away from its usual frenzied activity to a more receptive state, so that we can listen for what comes into it as soon as we seek the inner guidance.

Since Baba represents for me my true identity I try to remember to call on him repeatedly throughout the day, directing my attention to his human form in India, but also to his replica in my own heart. The more we remember to defer to him in this way, the closer we will come to uniting with who we really are. At first it is easier to think in terms of duality, as if the High Self is separate from us, until we have divested ourselves of the thick covering of thoughts, memories, superstitions, beliefs, habits, and all the rest of the accumulated barriers preventing our real Self from being able to express Itself through us. Eventually, we will be free to unite our will with Its will and become one whole Being.

Chapter 24

Practice What You Preach

Baba has frequently been heard to say that the main consideration in the application of his teachings is to bring the head, heart, and hands into harmony with one another so that our thinking, feeling, and acting all work together in any given situation. So many times we are made aware that these three functions are at odds with one another. Our heads can be filled with Baba's words, which we think are wonderful. But when we check our feelings we may discover that they are at variance with our thoughts, and when we take this investigation a step further we may be surprised and even horrified to find that we are acting quite differently, and at times even in opposition to our mental or emotional attitudes.

"Practice what you preach," we have been taught, yet so very few of us really do that. It is so easy to quote Baba's words, but to put them into practice is much more difficult for most people. We all lead such busy lives that we forget Baba's teachings despite the fact that we know with our minds that they are to be trusted and can safely be followed. But this knowledge has not yet communicated itself strongly enough to overcome all the multitudes of distractions and become imprinted on our memory as a habit. It takes practice, patience, and perseverance before we can really do as Baba asks: bring our thoughts, words, feelings, and deeds into line with his message.

It appears to be such a difficult task that he has given us smaller ones to prepare us for this major one, knowing full well that we have to take small steps before we are ready to move on to bigger ones. For, like babies, we cannot run before we crawl, however much we would like to and however hard we try.

This raises another important point. We cannot take even one step from the place where we wish we were, but only from where we actually are. So, to make progress possible complete honesty is necessary, not for anyone else's sake but for our own.

When we hear or read Baba's teachings we identify with what he says, but then the ego tries to persuade us that we are already putting them into practice. Yet, if we are strictly honest with ourselves, we are forced to admit that this is not altogether the case. We have become so success-oriented due to early training in competitiveness that we prefer to pretend that we are further along than we actually are. We all hate to fail.

One antidote to this self-deception is to remember that the only person in the whole world with whom we can really compare ourselves is our own self the way we were a week, a month, a year, or even longer ago. If we can honestly see an improvement in ourselves in the area we are considering, this knowledge will reassure us that we are progressing or developing and not standing still or stagnating. But to compare ourselves with anyone else is sheer folly, for the paths that led us to this present time and place were as different for each of us as the lessons we are here to learn.

So, the only sensible attitude we can adopt is one of strict honesty in examining our actions to judge whether they reflect what we really think, what we say, and what we feel. Only then will head, heart, and hands be aligned toward our goal.

Chapter 25

Direct Guidance

People often ask how they can begin to make more direct contact with their real Self in order to allow It to guide them in their everyday lives. Again, I can only share what has worked for me in the hope that it may be of help to others. Once, when I was meditating, I was given a formula composed of four words outlining the necessary steps for achieving closer identification with the Atma or High Self, enabling It to be the puppeteer with me as the puppet. The four words were *obedience*, *patience*, *concentration*, and *receptivity*, or keeping an open mind. As I thought about those four words I realized how perfectly they incorporated the necessary qualities we need to develop before we can expect to have closer contact with our real Selves.

We all lead such busy lives and have so little time for regular periods of meditation or quiet contemplation. However, it is not necessary to devote separate periods of long duration to succeed in making the desired inner contact. I recall the time I asked Baba if I should use a mantra for meditation and, if so, would he give me one. After first saying a firm "No," he elaborated by gently explaining that meditation should not be separate from other daily activities but should be practiced all day long. In that way we can gradually learn how to listen to the inner direction all the time instead of only during certain specified times of the day. He went on to suggest that we can link the natural action of breathing, which is continuous day and night and common to everyone, to this new habit of day-long meditating.

He then demonstrated this practice by humming aloud the syllable *so* as he inhaled, and by intoning the syllable *ham* as he exhaled. I started to copy him, but he quickly stopped me and cautioned me first to listen to him and then silently to hum them in my head without intoning them aloud. As his voice rose and fell in a definite rhythm it sounded like the waves breaking on the shore and seemed to link me to the universal pulse.

With daily practice this habit of quietly listening within will gradually produce the desired result of our being guided more and more by the Inner Mentor instead of by any outer authorities. However, it is a waste of time and energy to indulge in guilt if we forget it. It is much more beneficial to accept the fact that it was forgotten and immediately resume the practice. We all forget, but lamenting over a lapse is not necessary or productive.

Some of the early Christian saints referred to this daily listening as "practicing the presence." Whatever symbol is used to represent the High Self will provide the same result, for at that level all are one. Some people find that it helps to remain aware of the contact by silently repeating the name of the symbol or personification they have elected to use to represent It. The details are not important as the main purpose is to be consciously aware of our own True Identity. The four key words I received—obedience, patience, concentration, and receptivity, or "open-ness"— can act as a guide in this daily practice.

Obedience, for many of us, brings to mind the many times we heard the word spoken by our parents or other authority figures when we were children, and how we were sometimes too severely punished when we failed to obey the rules they had set for us. But obedience, when applied in this context, is not being requested of us by some outer authority but by our own Self, who is the best judge of what we need and what we should be doing. So any rebellious feelings this word raises are not really appropriate, for when we choose to be obedient to the directions we receive from our real Self, we can relax and let go of all the old feelings of insecurity, indecision, rebellion, and guilt.

Patience is a quality lacking in most of us, especially at this present time of hectic activity. It has also been undermined by the demand for instant gratification of our desires, instant healing, and either instant solutions to problems or instant escape from dealing with them by means of chemical or other kinds of addictions. But timing is of the utmost importance. There is a right time for everything to happen. If we try to use our will and desire to forcibly bring about instant results in a vain attempt to hasten the process, we will fail. We may even decide to give up our daily practice because we are unable to see any tangible results. But we may be just at the point when our efforts are about to produce observable progress, if only we can patiently continue them.

I remember when Baba illustrated this point with one of his little dramatized stories. He recounted an incident when a certain man had been given a task by his master to help him develop qualities that he lacked. The task was to break a huge rock into two parts by using a hammer. Baba described the efforts of the man to wield the hammer, which he did quite enthusiastically at first, but gradually lost interest until he finally gave up his efforts in despair of ever succeeding in breaking the huge rock. After some time, the master returned to inspect the man's progress only to find him sitting idle and disconsolate beside the rock, which was still intact. The master took the hammer and with one swift blow split the rock into two parts, to the astonishment of the man. The master then explained that he had stopped his attempt to split the rock just one hammer blow short of success.

Baba then turned to the group sitting around him at that interview. Gently but sadly he pointed out to those assembled in front of him that we were all like the man in the story. We were so impatient to see the results of our efforts that we stopped working on a project just as it was about to show the effects of our labor. We would be foolish to give up the practice of seeking the inner direction because we can see no appreciable results after a short time, since, like the man in Baba's story, if we were to continue with our daily practice the very next day could possibly bring about the desired contact and guidance we are seeking.

Concentration is also essential to success. Our monkey mind will try to interfere with the daily practice of meditation by introducing all kinds of extraneous distractions to seduce us. A method I learned many years ago when we were visiting a meditation center in Rangoon, Burma, and were under the tutelage of the presiding Mahasi Sayadaw, or head Monk, has proved to be extremely helpful in maintaining the required concentration. The meditation practice alternated between sitting for twenty minutes and walking for twenty minutes, but in a specific and very slow way. While sitting we were instructed to keep our attention on the air as it was breathed in through our nostrils and out again. Our attention would often wander at the beginning of the period, but after a short time the intervals between periods of distraction gradually diminished as we persevered, which greatly increased our ability to concentrate. In the walking meditation our attention was focused on the very slow deliberate movement of each leg as it was lifted up, stretched out in front of us, and gently lowered to the ground. This too was a tremendous help in fixing our attention on one act at a time.

Baba suggests the use of a candle flame to achieve a similar improvement in our powers of concentration. He likens the flame to the spark of Divinity we all carry within us. He says that by making a habit of meditating on the flame we will eventually become one with It.

Finally, we need to be *Receptive* or have an open mind in order to be able to receive insights from that same spark within us. If we have any resistance to being taught from this unseen source of wisdom, or if we still cling to our own opinions, ideas, preferences, or any other blocks to being open to fresh input, we will prevent the direct connection with the spark.

We need to develop the attitude of "Thy will, not mine, be done," and gradually learn to surrender all our own desires, trust that we will be given what is best for our growth, and become sufficiently open to accept whatever we encounter on our path, whether we approve of it or not. The experience of many people has shown that we can learn from everything that happens to us and from everyone who enters our life. But this is true only if we ask to be shown what they each have to teach us and, instead of complaining about how hard the lessons are, attend to the immediate task at hand, which is applying the knowledge and experience we gain in a practical way in our own lives.

By opening up our minds to the fullest extent to input—not only from our daily experiences but more importantly from the High Self—we will hasten our progress toward the goal of wholeness and balance. Eventually the Divine Puppeteer and our puppet personality will become one.

I am yours,
You are mine,
You are a tendril
I am the vine.

I am the parent,
You are the child
Sometimes obedient
But often wild.

I am the sun,
You are a ray
Hidden at night,
Effulgent by day.

I am the ocean,
You are a fish,
Out of my vastness
I grant what you wish.

I am in everything
And in each one of you.
In some I am visible
Though in only a few.

In many I'm hidden,
Deep down out of sight,
Until it is time
For my spark to ignite.

So blow on the ember
Which waits in your heart,
And I give you my promise
That I'll do my part.

You will find the whole world
Will come to your aid
If you work very hard
'Till your karma is paid.

Since I am in all things
Why do you still doubt?
Since I exist everywhere
You can't shut me out.

So choose to take hold
Of this wonderful chance
To join with me
In the cosmic dance,

When each of you grasps
My myriad hands,
Not just in India
But in all other lands.

As I am the Avatar
Of the whole world scene,
Wake up to reality
And out of your dream.

Chapter 26

Love My Uncertainty

It is my perception—drawn from listening to many people relate their personal histories—that insecurity is the most common underlying cause for the majority of the problems from which we suffer. So we need to find a remedy for this condition if we hope to be able to make Practical Spirituality our way of life.

Such widespread insecurity is understandable when we consider the manifold symbols of hoped-for security that people strive to attain, none of which are lasting and therefore can guarantee no permanent security. The more they strive to attain some measure of the security they crave the further it recedes, like a will-o'-the-wisp, forever beyond their reach.

Different individuals express insecurity in various ways according to their supposed needs. Some people think they will feel secure if they find the perfect partner, while others concentrate on securing a safe occupation, or a certain amount of money to provide them with the secure feeling they seek. Still others may believe that they can achieve their goal as soon as they attain a degree from an accepted college, or are promoted to an important and influential position at work or in the community where they live. So many people are desperately trying to find that magical and mystical state where they will feel safe and secure.

Our heritage, our education, the opinions and values current in the world around us, all point to specific panaceas for this chronic disease. We are persuaded by the media that if we buy a particular product or attain a specific goal that we will feel satisfied and fulfilled, but the reverse is the inevitable result and we are forced to look further and more feverishly for that illusive state of security.

As this situation persists, more and more people are exhibiting signs of insecurity in their behavior, both consciously and unconsciously. Their attitude is the result of a desire to convince others, but primarily themselves, of their own value, ability, prowess, knowledge, importance, attractiveness, or whatever other proof of their superiority they can accept as convincing. Often this attitude means that they are protesting too much—they assume the role of being utterly secure and sure of themselves when, actually, such an attitude is no more than a mask to conceal their self-doubt. Some people resort to the cruel habit of criticizing others to boost their own importance, skill, brilliance, or other attribute in the eyes of the victim, but also to reassure themselves of their own superiority. Others will openly reveal their lack of confidence and self-esteem in a bid for reassurance from others that they are worthy of approval, since they themselves have no confidence in their own value. Yet others will consort with those whom they consider to be important in some way, in the erroneous belief that it will reflect onto them and give them a borrowed sense of security. Such are the hangers-on who gather around famous people, hoping to ride to fame or fortune on their coattails. These are just a few of the many ways people fool themselves in an effort to overcome the gnawing feeling that insecurity causes.

But what actually is security? Is it so important or worth all the effort expended to attain it? And why is it always beyond our reach despite every effort to achieve it? The answer lies in yet another question that Baba repeatedly urges us to ask ourselves: "Who Am I?" He supplies the answer in many different ways, usually by showing us what we are not. For, when we have discarded all the things we are not, we can be free to discover who we *are*, for Baba assures us that we are all God. But this assertion is far too difficult for most people to believe, for they are accustomed to identifying themselves with their physical body-mind-personality-ego complex, forgetting that it is merely the container for the real Self.

Insecurity is completely unnecessary; in fact, it is a futile waste of time and energy, simply because people have sought their security in the wrong direction—in the outer world instead of within themselves. If we expect it to be granted to us by attachment to anyone or anything outside ourselves we are doomed to disappointment. It can only be found when we identify ourselves with who we really are: the unseen Spark within the outer observable sheath in which we exist in the world, and which is of equal value to the Spark in everyone else. So, where is the need for insecurity if we are all equal in value? And why do we try to be "better" than anyone else?

Our heritage and early conditioning are the cause of our mistaken identity and the resulting insecurity that it causes. We have been taught in each new birth into this world to identify ourselves with our physical bodies and our attendant thoughts, feelings, speech, acts, desires, and senses. We have all been taught untruths about our true identity from the very beginning of our many sojourns on earth, resulting in the haunting sense of insecurity from which we have all continuously suffered. In each succeeding life we have continued to seek security, only to be left even more insecure by having failed to find it. Many people have been driven to depression, insanity, and even suicide by the failure of their search. In each new age the situation has worsened as this pattern becomes more deeply etched on the human mind. The resulting dejection leads to even more control by the monkey mind in its search for security.

Now the time is approaching for a new and very different way of life to be ushered in, heralded in large part by Baba's life and ministry. In the coming New Age we shall all be taught who we really are, and our erstwhile hidden identity will be revealed to everyone so we can learn to feel secure in the knowledge that we all are equal in our God-selves, none better or worse, wiser or more stupid, stronger or weaker, richer or poorer, but all one and of equal value at the common source. But in order to move more freely into this new and very different way of life, relying more and more on our inner Reality to direct us, we will need to detach ourselves from all the old false and disappointing pseudo-security symbols and replace them with the only security that is permanent—identification with our real Self—which is perfect and therefore completely trustworthy.

Some of us will undoubtedly be pioneers and make the first leap in faith from the known to the as-yet-unknown, where none of the old rules and codes of behavior will be of any use and where there will be no certainty of what will happen at any given moment. None of our own plans will be valued, only those that are initiated and then directed by the source of wisdom within each one of us. It will mean giving up the known, and we all dislike having to face the unknown. Many people even prefer a familiar situation that is painful to an unknown future where there are no familiar ground rules to follow, only the direction of the High Self to guide us one minute at a time. This is the place where Baba is seeking to lead us and it is the main reason he says he has assumed human form at this time of great need. So he urges us to "love my uncertainty," which is the cure for the insecurity we have all suffered so long.

Beloved Baba hear my wish
Which I address to thee,
To fill me up so full of you
There's no room left for me.

Beloved Baba take my life
And shape it as you will,
And then please live it through me,
Your wishes to fulfill.

Beloved Baba give me strength
And take away all fear
As you have proved that you can do
Throughout this troubled year.

Beloved Baba take my heart
And make of it your home.
And you will be installed in it
Wherever I may roam.

Chapter 27

Why Fear When I Am Here?

Another of Baba's favorite sayings is, "Why fear when I am here?" He then adds, "I am your near and dear." He also tells us that we are all part of the vast God-force in which we are immersed like fish in water. So that must mean that God is not only inside us but also around us, since It is what supports all life and so all living creatures.

I remember as a child being told that God was above, below, in front, behind, and at either side of us. But such a statement only confused me, and since it was never adequately explained but only referred to as one of the mysteries, I remained confused even into adulthood. I remember looking around to see if I could catch a glimpse of God out of the corner of my eye but, of course, never did. No one even so much as hinted that my own real Self was God. That would have been considered sacrilege at the time when I was growing up in England, but many changes are now taking place. What a comfort it is to be told that this is true even though we may be unaware of this basic truth because we have accumulated so many layers of conditioning that cover the spark of Divinity and keep it buried out of sight deep within us all.

Another saying I heard the minister of the church we attended pronounce with great regularity in his sermons was, "The kingdom of heaven is within you," and yet another that followed naturally, "Seek ye first the kingdom of heaven and all things shall be added unto you." But how, I used to wonder, was that to be attained? Baba answers that question by advising us to develop the habit of deferring to the spark of Divinity within us and seeking

Its help in discarding the layers that have built up around It during our many sojourns on the Earth in human bodies. The more we turn our attention away from all the outer distractions that beckon our monkey minds to become attached and then trapped by them, the more aware we will become of who we really are. And the more we develop this habit, the easier it will be to practice it regularly.

We have so completely identified ourselves with the outer trappings—our bodies, brains, egos, wills, and personalities—that we have come to believe that they are our real Selves. So we cater to them to try to keep them happy and satisfied, which is a never-ending task and doomed to failure. For, like everything else in tangible form, they too are unreliable and will fail us by becoming ill, depressed, doubting, angry, and all the other changes that the physical form is heir to when we most need their support.

As soon as we understand that the physical and mental package is not real or reliable, and turn for support to the Reality residing within it and stop trying to force our will to acquire or achieve specific goals, "all things will be added unto" us. The result could be, and often is, even more fulfilling than we would ever have dreamed possible, and probably more than we think we could ever deserve to be given.

However, just because we have espoused Baba's teachings does not necessarily mean that we will be free from problems, sorrows, traumas, fears, or any other of life's experiences, as I most certainly have learned. Baba does not wave a magic wand and make all our problems disappear. Instead, by teaching us that we are all God, he gives us the very means with which to handle any crises by relying on the only truly trustworthy force in the world to help us to accept whatever occurs. By surrendering to It, we can open the way to be shown the solution. In other words, "Why fear when I am here?" as Baba so often asks us.

So we need to let go of our own preferences, supposed needs, and false securities and surrender our lives to the guidance of the High Self, rely on It as the only force we can safely trust to know our real needs, and be willing to accept whatever It decides to bring about. This kind of action can be the start of a new way of living whereby we will be lived through by the High Self instead of in the old habitual way of trying to use force with our will to achieve whatever we want. This new way of living is so much more relaxing. After it has become a little more familiar as a way of life, and therefore easier to follow, it is much more of a challenge and an adventure. However, this is not intended to imply that we should lean back and do nothing. We will probably find we are actually accomplishing far more than we ever imagined was possible, but are no longer tense or exhausted from the effort.

Chapter 28

Let Go and Let God

As a small child, I frequently heard the minister of our church end his Sunday sermon with the admonition, "Let go and let God." This injunction was never explained to me, or if it was not in a way that I—as a child—could understand. So I had no idea what it meant and even less how to put it into practice. What should I let go of, I often wondered, and what should I let God do?

Baba has stated what we should do very clearly. "Your first duty is to abandon. Abandon all your plans, even the best ones. Abandon all the theories you cherish, the doctrines you hold dear, the systems of knowledge which have cluttered your brain, the preferences you have accumulated, the pursuit of fame, fortune, scholarship, superiority. These are all material, objective. Enter into the objective world after becoming aware of the Atma. Then you will realize that all is the play of the Atma."

Many people react to the idea of "letting go and letting God" with fear and trepidation. They labor under the delusion that God is some powerful authority outside themselves and separate from them, so they are afraid of being controlled by an outer force or figure. But Baba teaches that this concept of separateness from God is erroneous. He assures us that we are all God, but that we have separated ourselves from God by forgetting our true identity rather than the other way around—God separating Himself from us—which can never happen.

So when we consider the statement, "Let go and let God," we are actually letting go of our ego and its attachment to all it holds dear, and allowing our true Self to be expressed through our personality, which It will do only if we ask It to. This situation is the opposite of domination, for it leaves us completely free to decide who should guide our lives: our ego/personality or our God-Self? Which is the more reliable? Obviously the God-Self—which is universal, knows all, and is the core of our being—is the only reliable Mentor and Guide.

So, we need to begin the habit of deferring to this inner mentor as often as possible and particularly in situations where we feel insecure about how to act. Again, as with all good intentions, we so often forget. When we do, we need to be patient with ourselves instead of depressed, guilty, or harshly self-critical. It is best to pick ourselves up, dust ourselves off, and start all over again.

I wish I were a little moth
Attracted to your flame
To let it burn away from me
All else except your name.

I wish I were a little flower
Wide open to your sun
To follow you around all day
Until its end has come.

I wish I were a butterfly
Atop your lotus feet,
Sipping your amrita
To make its life complete.

I wish I were a little bird
Which sings its heart away,
Repeating constantly your name
From morn till night each day.

But I am really none of these,
And yet I'm all of them,
For the spark of life in all that lives
Is the same in women and men.

And all the sparks together
Add up to one great whole,
Which is the God we worship
Reflected in each soul.

So I can be a little moth
Attracted to your flame,
And let it burn away from me
All else except your name.

Chapter 29

Be Happy

Baba often tells a person, and sometimes a whole assembly of people, "Be happy." It is such a simple little command, yet to many people it is confusing and frustrating and extremely difficult to follow. They are then likely to give up in resignation and lapse back into their old habits of complaining, mourning, criticizing, judging, and all the other negative mental pursuits in which the mind is eager to engage unless it is employed in some useful activity.

It is a distressing fact that the majority of people today are not merely not happy, but are acutely unhappy. Like the monkey with its fist filled with nuts, caught inside the bottle, we are equally trapped by our own thoughts, desires, and reactions. And also like the monkey, we too prefer to lay the blame on someone or something other than ourselves, not realizing that we are free to choose how we react. We can either hold on to our black moods or let go of what we thought we wanted but did not get, which is usually the cause of the negative thoughts in the first place.

As in the illustration of the black and white birds, we tend to want to push away those things we fear or do not want to happen, and grab hold of those things we crave or fear we will not achieve. It is easy to see that fear is the most common underlying emotion in either of these situations. It is also frequently the cause of negative reactions such as anger, depression, and other types of unhappiness. "Be happy" is often just as difficult to put into practice as "Why fear when I am here?" Yet the two are closely connected, for we are depressed or unhappy because we fear that something we do not want to happen will, or that something we hope for will not come to pass.

So both fear and unhappiness, as well as all other kinds of negativity, can be traced back to the monkey mind and the belief that someone or something outside ourselves is causing our problems and our negative reactions, when, in fact, we can either choose to allow ourselves to be made unhappy, or to detect what it is we are continuing to hold on to for our imagined security and then let it go. If we would only let go of whatever the false security may be we could be free, just as the monkey could escape from entrapment and eventual capture if it would only open its tightly clasped fist and let go of the fruit, nuts, or other delicacies held so tightly in it.

Baba represents for us in human form, our Higher Self. So "Why fear when I am near?" literally means, why do we fear when the wise and loving Self that we really are is available within us to give us all we need? For "closer is He than breathing, and nearer than hands and feet." ["The Higher Pantheism," vi. From the Oxford Dictionary of Quotations (London & New York: Oxford University Press, 1955.)] But we have to be willing to let go of what we think we need in order to be open to receive what It is waiting to give us.

Baba says, "Be happy," but how can we possibly be happy if we are full of fear? It is obvious that we must let go of the reason for our fear in order to be happy. But the cause of our fear is our identification with the body and its senses, which lure the monkey mind to seek its hoped-for security from outer attachments instead of from within by serving the Higher Self as Hanuman had learned to serve Rama. Since we all have free choice we need to find ways to help us choose what will provide lasting happiness without any fear attached to it, for this way lies true freedom.

So how does our monkey mind, led out of control by the five senses, keep us trapped in unhappiness and fear?

One of the chief ways is by allowing ourselves to sink down into depression and hopelessness, which leaves us feeling utterly helpless and reinforces our belief that there is no escape. However, this does not mean we should be a Pollyanna and play the role of being happy or pretend to be content and free from fear, for that is the way of self-deception. Perseverance and discipline are needed to keep turning within and away from all the outer distractions and to follow Hanuman's example of constantly seeking ways to serve Rama or the High Self.

Merrily, merrily go your way
Wearing a smile as you live each day.
I will fill you full of love
So act with the softness of a dove.

Then you can temper the sword in your hand
Which I will use to cleanse the land.
Keep close contact daily with me
And I will be always with thee.

Chapter 30

Monkey or Human?

There is another aspect of the monkey mind. Baba has said that we share the instincts and senses and everything else connected to the physical body with animals and other living creatures. But, unlike animals, human beings are also endowed with characteristics not shared by other species. He tells us that we alone are able to feel that we are different from the body, and we alone are capable of discrimination and intelligence and are able to control our senses. He explains that we are moving up the evolutionary ladder from the animal level to that of the animal/human, then to fully human, human/Divine, and finally to fully Divine, which is our true identity.

To attempt this climb we need to take the necessary steps to leave behind the purely animal part of our nature by ceasing to identify ourselves with our body and the scores of appetites that further attach us to it. "You are not the body," Baba repeatedly cautions us, yet we still allow it to control us instead of retaining control over it. To that extent we sentence ourselves to remain at the animal/human level, unable to proceed up the evolutionary ladder to eventual union or identification with the Divine, which is the state we understand as enlightenment.

The more we allow the mind to lure us to follow the senses and—by behaving like animals—descend the ladder instead of ascending it, we will be guilty of hindering our own progress. The vast majority of us here now in the *Kali Yuga* live and act more like monkeys even though we have the opportunity of becoming increasingly human. It is natural for a monkey to act like an animal controlled by its five senses, but not *dharmic* for a human being to do so. We should aspire to become more and more godlike by constantly deferring to the spark of Divinity within the physical shell It animates.

Chapter 31

Keep It Simple

Many times Baba can be heard saying in his soft and re-assuring voice, "Keep it simple." A common tendency appears to be to think that it is necessary and desirable to express Baba's teachings in as erudite a manner as possible for them to be impressive and attract people to practice them. Our motive for believing that this is necessary may be to impress others with our knowledge and gain their admiration, rather than from a desire to benefit others by sharing what we have learned in as simple a way as possible to ensure that the listeners understand.

I have always had a tendency to overestimate other people's knowledge or expertise and at the same time underestimate my own abilities. In recent years, however, I have learned that the more simply and clearly something is expressed the more likely it will be for more people to comprehend the meaning and then be willing and able to take the next step to put it into practice, which is the most important part of any learning. We have to be like little children to enter the kingdom of heaven! If we are caught up in intellectualizing we are less likely to practice what we preach. Baba himself uses very simple directions and illustrations as well as a great deal of repetition to ensure that by repeating a point he wishes to make many times in slightly different ways, his message will be received and understood by the maximum number of people. We have all listened to speakers whose language and delivery were superb, but the content of their lecture was lost to most of the audience. When asked to report on what was said,

the listeners invariably have to admit that they cannot remember.

Spiritual "snobbery," in addition to every other kind,
must be eliminated, for it is one of the biggest stumbling
blocks on the inner journey to the Self. Instead of wasting
time in a vain endeavor to impress others with our knowledge or ability, we could help ourselves and others by
sharing what we have learned as simply and concisely as
possible. It is the information we are sharing, not our own
importance, that is of value to other people, so the more
simply it is expressed the greater the number of people
who will be given an opportunity to benefit from it.

We all have similar problems, yet many of us feel that
we alone have certain specific ones, so it is a comfort to
hear that others share them. In addition, it is a great help
to hear other people relate the different ways in which we
can help ourselves and also—by being willing to share our
own insights—allow others to use ideas we have found to
be helpful. I always think of this activity as cross-polli-
nation.

To either overrate or underrate ourselves or others is
foolish, for we are all equal as far as our real Self is concerned. It is only our personalities that are different, de-
pending on what we still need to learn. Comparison is also
limiting and a sheer waste of time and energy. It is preferable and more practical to realize that we all have problems to work out in this life and that we have specific
lessons to learn according to our karma, so it is useless to
compare ourselves with anyone else. The only valid comparison is between ourselves the way we used to be and
the way we are now to determine whether we have learned
from our mistakes and made any real progress.

I love you all every single one,
For deep within I see,
Beneath the ego layers,
Your own Divinity.

No one of you is special
Or more lovable to me,
For each of you possesses
Your own Divinity.

So don't compete with others
To seek security,
When my love you have already
From your own Divinity.

Direct my love to others
Who are blind and cannot see,
The love they seek so desperately
Is their own Divinity.

For as you seek in everyone
The counterpart of me,
You'll start to open up your hearts
To the one Divinity.

Chapter 32

My Life Is My Message

Baba frequently says that his life is his message, and that his teachings can be evaluated by the way he lives his life. He also says that we too should endeavor to make our lives his message and live our lives in tune with it. Anyone who has visited Baba at his ashram in India and observed even the comparatively small part of his daily schedule that is visible to visitors will agree that his daily routine is indeed his message, for it would be utterly impossible for any of us to do all that he accomplishes without effort and with so much love. He teaches us to be loving and to see only the innate God-Self in everyone, including ourselves. It is impossible to be around him and fail to feel the love he pours out every minute of the day to everyone who is open to receive it.

He advises us to do everything as an act of worship so that our lives will also reflect his message. But for many people this seems to be too vague to put into practice, and they say they do not know where to begin. We are all a mixture of good intentions but not always good actions. The best way to make the two consistent is to remember who we really are and ask the God-Self within to take charge and act through us in such a way that our lives will gradually become more and more in tune with Baba's message. But we all forget, even though we may be aware of the necessity of deferring to our real Self in this way and are convinced that It can change our behavior. Instead of despairing of ever being successful in such a practice, and perhaps giving up the attempt, we should take heed of the memory lapse and immediately remedy it by once again soliciting the help of the God-within to take over and guide our steps.

You are the only one,
You are in everyone,
You are the guiding star
Clearly seen wherever we are.

You are the heart's delight,
You are the inner light,
You are the charioteer,
You are the near and dear.

But we so oft forget,
We have not learned as yet
To put our trust in you,
And let you carry us through.

Whatever happens, be it good or bad,
However we're feeling, whether happy or sad,

You are not far away,
You're with us night and day,
You are so near and dear
We need not ever fear.

Praise to our Higher Self
Which is our only wealth,
We feel your perfect love
Flowing to us from above.

Chapter 33

No Hidden Agenda

Whether we are willing to admit it or not, we all dissemble. This is a trick we learned during childhood, born out of the fear of being punished. We say one thing but think something quite different, sometimes even contrary. A recent phrase that is being used for this situation is to "have a hidden agenda." *Two-faced* or *hypocritical* were terms used to describe it when I was a child. The outer face is designed to give the impression of going along with what others expect, but putting them off the scent so to speak, while the inner face reserves the right to our own opinion or plan. This is one of the ways the ego endeavors to retain control, yet makes it appear the opposite.

The outer attitude is false and acts as a red herring to distract others so we can achieve what the ego wants without opposition. Having deceived whoever was opposing us and our plan, we proceed to take them by surprise by revealing our hidden motive as soon as it is deemed safe to do so, or when it is already a *fait accompli*.

The need to have a hidden agenda or a false front stems from fear of opposition, ridicule, punishment, or failure. When it is a ploy to get our own way it is a form of dishonesty. It hides the real motive, which is to control the situation but deceive others into believing we are being forthright. A conman is an extreme example of this type of activity where the perpetrator gains the confidence of his victims by assuring them of his pure motives and promising them future gains if they will only trust him. As soon as he has won their confidence and they have acceded to his plan, he absconds with the funds he has wheedled out of them, leaving them penniless. Any such subterfuges or manipulations are dishonest, so we need to observe our behavior closely in order to catch sight of incidences of such dishonesty, of which we may heretofore have been completely unaware.

Chapter 34

You Are All Walking Temples

Baba will very often toss out a simple phrase. It's a hint for each of us to contemplate. We need to discover its meaning for us personally—a meaning that usually exists on many levels. He refuses to spoon-feed us but provides enough of a hint to entice us to figure out how to apply the concept to our lives. In one of his discourses, Baba said, "You are all walking temples," which was a new idea to many of us who were hearing it for the first time. The more I thought about it the more I realized how wonderfully appropriate it was.

So how can we apply this particular description of ourselves as walking temples and bring our lives into harmony with it? The story in the New Testament describing how Jesus cleared out the moneylenders who were desecrating the temple comes to mind. What is soiling or desecrating our temple? Is it our emotions, thoughts, desires, plans, habits, and all the other tendencies of the monkey mind we are still allowing to control us? Whatever soils our temple needs to be cleared away so the worship for which it was intended can take place.

The outside of the temple needs to be kept clean, too. Many devotees have the mistaken idea that to be "spiritual" means to be unkempt and unaware of their appearance, but that is not what Baba teaches. He encourages us to be spotlessly clean, well-groomed, and neatly and attractively dressed, but not in any way flamboyant.

Baba tells us that his life is his message and he says that our lives should express his message, too. He expects us to accept our station in life and to live within it as dharmically as possible. If we are pleasingly dressed and well-groomed, our friends and relatives, and others we meet will be more likely to want to know more about us and our way of life. If, on the other hand, we look like beggars, they will be less interested. Even more importantly, we will attract more people to Baba's teachings if we demonstrate his teachings on a daily basis in our activities and relationships. By being honest in our dealings with others, correct in our behavior, loving in our relationships, at peace with ourselves, willing to refrain from negative thoughts, feelings, words and actions, we can best advertise his message. And that message is that we are all walking temples!

Beloved Baba, take this shell
Do with it what you will,
For I'm profoundly tired of it
When it's so often ill.

Beloved Baba, take this shell
And use it as a glove
In which to put your little hand
To fill me with your love.

Beloved Baba, take this shell.
I give it back to you,
For only you know what it is
Through me you wish to do.

Beloved Baba, take this shell
And make it fit for you
To dwell in as a temple
Where I can worship you.

Chapter 35

Find Me in Your Heart

Perhaps one of the most important reasons for Baba to have chosen to incarnate in human form at this time is to teach us that we are all aspects of the Universal God-force. He has said, "Yes, I say that I am God, but finish the quotation. I also tell you that you too are all God. The only difference between us is that I know I am God and you do not yet know that." Following that assurance, he teaches us that we should not become attached to his form any more than we should seek security in the tangible form of anything or anyone else in the outer world. Instead, he urges us to find his counterpart or replica in our own heart. In that way we will become Self-dependent, Self-sufficient, Self-confident, and Self-motivated.

But this undertaking seems to be one of the most difficult for most people to accept. We hear his words with our ears when we are with him at his ashram, and we see them printed on paper as we read his discourses with our eyes, yet many still cling to the desire to have him personally answer our questions, give us specific directions, reassure us that we are good devotees, and, most of all, approve whatever plan or dream we may be entertaining at any particular time.

But to be attached to his form does not allow us to be free to seek within for direction from our own God-Self. If we continue to expect him to tell us what to do and what not to do, we will remain at the emotional level of children who are still attached to their parents beyond a reasonable age. If the parents are unavailable when advice is needed— or if they have died—the grown child is lost and unsure of how to proceed, completely incapable of making any decisions.

In exactly the same way, we need to be weaned from Baba's form if we are ever to learn to rely on his counterpart within us. We will be useless to Baba and his mission unless we have matured to the point where we are guided from within more and more of the time. Baba needs independent people whom he can trust to act according to his teachings, and in that way attract others to his message by allowing him to live through them.

You never believe me though you think you do.
You are too busy wondering what to do.
You ask me and ask me, but never listen.
I tell you and tell you that it is my mission
To seek you and draw you and teach you the truth,
Or as much as I know you can use.
Do not ask for too much or ask not at all
But trust me to give you your dues.

Chapter 36

From Generation to Generation

We are all born into an already existing family, to two parents whose long line of ancestors stretches back into the past for many generations. We take from this vast stock-pile of attributes, tendencies, assets, gifts, weaknesses, characteristics, and even illnesses, whatever we need to give us the greatest opportunity to learn what we failed to learn in any of our prior lives. We do not need all the tendencies available from either of these sources, only those that fit our individual karmic lessons. Thus, several children born to the same two parents and who have inherited different tendencies from the same two lines of ancestors, can be very different from the other siblings and even from the parents themselves.

We do not enter this life as a blank slate ready to be written on. We trail behind us the effects of many other lives and the accumulation of both positive and negative qualities that form the foundation on which the present life is built. But at present, people are not content with the slow and automatic process of working out their karma with the help of the family into which they were born and the heritage extending back in time on both sides. Many individuals are becoming aware that they can hasten the process by asking themselves how they can consciously learn the lessons their present family setting has given them and accept the opportunity to understand and learn from these lessons. This accelerates the process and renders the inherited conditions no longer necessary or helpful as soon as the learning they allowed has taken place.

But many of the old habits are still active and, like all

habits, die hard. Instead of being helpful, they can easily hinder those who have made the decision to work consciously on themselves to further their progress toward the chosen goal of allowing the High Self to live and breathe through them. Old habits hold them back just as effectively as if they were in chains, which indeed they are, for they are bound to the chain reactions of the many past generations to which they are attached by being born to their present parents. Many people express a feeling of being held back and not free to move ahead, as if they are chained to the past. In such instances these chains need to be cut so that these individuals can move ahead with their tasks, free from their restraint.

Each life offers us the opportunity to break free from these chain reactions designed to enable us to take the necessary steps to gain release from our karma. We all have this opportunity in our present life if we have diligently worked through the tests it presented or imposed upon us. But some people have become so accustomed to being held back and frustrated, they are afraid to let go and face the unknown future free from these chains. They often present many different excuses in a vain attempt to explain why they hesitate to break free. They will say they are still too attached to outer security symbols such as money, possessions, relationships, or their own success, as if they were being asked to relinquish any of these. It is not these things themselves that need to be given up but the imagined security derived from them, which is no security at all.

Usually, those who realize the advantage they can derive from being released from their past heritage have already arrived at the place where they have experienced for themselves how meaningless life can be, unless they move on instead of remaining tied to restraints that are no longer relevant. Once we have come to the conclusion that nothing we achieve with our own will is lasting or capable of providing permanent satisfaction, we will begin to realize that there is nothing left to us except to move ahead, free to be lived through by our real Self instead of being ego-motivated as we have been in the past.

I closed the trap doors long ago
To contact with my soul.
In many lives since then I've tried
To seek afresh my goal.

But now I've met that shining one
Who has the power to aid,
I seek again with newfound strength
For which I've dearly paid.

So now I pray with all my heart
That he who knows my goal
Will help me keep wide open
The doorway to my soul.

I will hold back no longer
For time is slipping by,
And I desire to see the light
To guide me when I die.

You promise if we take one step
To meet us ten you'll take.
So Baba, from my heart I pray
This union I can make.

Chapter 37

When the Pupil Is Ready

We often hear or read the phrase, "When the pupil is ready, the master will appear." But why do we need a master at all? I, along with many others, have often asked this question. When I first went to see Baba, it really bothered me. I had been taught in the work I do to rely only on my inner source of wisdom. I continued to worry about this question despite the tremendous attraction I was feeling toward Baba. Then quite unexpectedly one day, I came to the realization that he represents in human form the High Self within each of our human forms. From that time I have had no further problem.

Some people are able to conceive of the High Self as formless, but the majority of people find it much easier to make contact with a living, breathing, walking person who can remind us all that we, too, are gods at the core of our being. So Baba is here to teach us by setting an example of how to behave as he ignites with his energy and love the spark of Divinity within each one of us. It can then burn brightly as a flame or a lamp to light our way, as well as to provide others with a signpost for their inner journey. But as soon as this has happened, he starts to wean us away from dependence on his form, exactly as all animal and bird mothers wean their young as soon as their offspring are sufficiently developed to fend for themselves and gradually become more and more independent.

So the actual time when we first meet Baba or other teachers is most significant. As soon as we are open to be taught, the right teacher will appear, as if magnetically drawn to us and we to the teacher.

But we are all in such a hurry in this modern world in which we live that many people watch the clock all day long, worried that there will not be sufficient time in which to accomplish the many activities scheduled for each day.

While driving on freeways we are made acutely aware of cars weaving in and out of the lines of traffic, often dangerously close to the car ahead or the one they want to pass in their desperate effort to save a few minutes. When the traffic is extremely congested, with hundreds of cars creeping along bumper-to-bumper, the stress level of many of the drivers rises alarmingly and they sound their horns or try to cut into a lane that appears to be moving faster than the one they are in. Because of the increasing difficulty to travel at the prescribed speed due to such congestion, it is hard to gauge the amount of time required for each journey, especially at the peak hours in the early morning and late afternoon when most commuters are driving to and from their place of work.

This supposed need to speed filters into all areas of life, including the inner path in search of identity. We all tend to look for a quick fix, a magic wand, or instant control or gratification, all of which energizes our monkey mind. But all the ancient traditions emphasize that there is a time for everything and that it is this right timing that we should all follow, rather than the outer clock time. On one of our trips to see Baba, I was wearing a watch with no numbers on its face to indicate the hours. Baba spied it on my wrist and came up to me. Pointing to it, he said, "Very good. Inner time, not clock time."

On the purely mundane level, it is obvious that it will take a certain length of time for a fruit to ripen, a flower to bloom, or a child to learn to walk. If we eat the fruit before it is ripe a stomachache will result. If we pick a flower while it is still a tight bud it cannot open fully. If we try to force a child to walk before its muscles and sense of balance are developed it will fall. These are small examples, but we are all sometimes guilty of trying to force growth at a faster rate than is possible or safe. It is the same when we set forth on an inner journey to the Self. We are all in such a hurry to attain enlightenment in one big leap, not realizing that it will happen only when the time is right and we have learned to defer to the High Self and eventually merge with it.

Baba is so tuned in to each of us, since he represents our true Self, that he can detect instantly what we need at any particular moment to further our progress and development. We may be under the impression that we are ready and that he should speak to us, but only he knows what we really need. Because he is identical to the Universal God-force we can trust him and, above all, trust his timing, which is accurate whereas ours is not.

I love to watch you use your hands
So delicate and small,
Especially when your cymbals mark
The bhajan's rise and fall.

They look like little spirits
With a life style all their own,
As they dance with joy to hear you sing
And gaily mark each tone.

At times one hand will hover
Like a bird poised in midair,
And everyone will wonder
If the answer to a prayer

Will suddenly be visible,
As it circles round and round,
Then pounces quick to catch the gift
Before it hits the ground.

Will it be vibhuti
To ease some person's pain?
Or will it be a talisman,
Reminding them to call your name?

Whenever they're in trouble,
And their faith begins to fade,
So that you will be alerted
To hurry to their aid?

And then at times like butterflies
They unexpectedly alight
On head or hand or heart or arm
To ease a sufferer's plight.

So many people touch your feet
And press on them a kiss
But let us not forget your hands.
They too confer your bliss.

Chapter 38

A Rose by Any Other Name

One of the means Baba gives us to overcome the monkey mind is to repeat one of the many names by which God is known in various parts of the world. By occupying the mind this daily discipline will—at the same time—teach us to be constantly aware of our true identity and show us where our real security is to be found. However, the various names and forms attributed to God by people from many different heritages can pose a problem—as the long history of religious wars testifies—when each side firmly believes their God to be the only true name and form. But we must bear in mind the fact that the actual God-force existing everywhere in the universe is not limited to any one form or one name. The chosen name by which we address God, or the form we attribute to It, and the name and form used to represent It in other cultures, are all valid for those who choose to make contact with this formless and nameless energy that sustains the universe.

Many religious groups in the past were obviously aware of the trap that naming or portraying God could be for the unwary. So, to replace the specific names they used symbols that carry in one design or form an entire message, all of which is understood by the subconscious mind. For example, two distinct flowers have long been in use as symbols for the spark of Divinity within each of us known as the spirit, soul, and many other terms. In the West the rose has usually been the preferred symbol, while in the East the lotus is more often used.

The rose has many appealing characteristics, chief among them being its fragrance, which persists even after the flower has died. The fallen petals have been used for centuries to make attar of roses to perfume clothing, closets, and rooms with their continuing essence. The fact that the rose has thorns that protect it from marauders is also significant. Our real Self is protected deep within us and permeates every cell of our being with its essence but is unapproachable until we are ready to recognize it. By removing the many thorns of our negative personality traits we can approach the perfect Self we have always been and allow Its fragrance to perfume our life. The rose within everyone is exactly the same—and just as sweet—and would continue to be so by whatever name it was called. As Gertrude Stein pointed out, "A rose is a rose, is a rose, is a rose."

The lotus, the flower more frequently used as a symbol for the indwelling God in the East, expresses in a different way the same meaning. The lotus is rooted in the mud at the bottom of the pond in which it grows. A pond is frequently used as a symbol of the subconscious mind, which carries forgotten memories, emotions, and experiences—both positive and negative in content. The lotus pushes its way up through the water into the air where it unfolds in the light of the sun, its pure flower unsullied by the mud from which it has risen.

If a rose by any other name would smell as sweet, as Shakespeare affirms in *Romeo and Juliet*, why wouldn't the same apply to God when addressed by one of the many names used throughout the world? We have a choice and can use whatever name we prefer to repeat when we seek to engage the monkey mind in a perpetual activity to wean it away from its attachment to security symbols in the external world of form.

Baba also tells us to visualize the form of our chosen symbol of God. But here again many questions arise, just as they do with the repetition of the name. Most of the names belong to Beings no longer in human form. But Baba is very much alive and in a tangible form for all to see. However, he tells us not to be attached to his form but only to what it symbolizes: the Self within each of our hearts. The human tendency is to rely on a form to make the object of worship more real until an abstract concept of God as energy can be accepted.

Baba's antidote for the monkey mind is to keep turning away from the outer world to the Resident in our hearts by using whatever name we choose to call It and by whatever form we wish to visualize it. Those of us who have come under Baba's tutelage find it natural to use his name and form, but he avers that it is not necessary for everyone to use the same ones. The only important thing to remember is to practice this method. Baba often illustrates turning within by saying that we have been given a key. If we turn the key one way we are attached to the world with all its temporary security symbols, and if we turn the key the other way we connect ourselves to our real Self. It is up to us which way we choose to turn it.

So let us do as Baba advises and abandon all the plans our egos have presented to us. This is the recipe for practical spirituality that will help to overcome or tame the monkey mind. Then we can be like Hanuman, a servant to Rama, or any other name we choose to represent the God we really are. If just a few people in the world would adopt this practice, hope for a new world order would not be so impossible a dream.

For many lifetimes I have tried,
As each new life I entered,
To do those tasks allotted me,
But I was too self-centered.

As I look back I clearly see
How foolish I have been,
For how could I expect success
While living in a dream?

When I awoke and realized
That life was more than this,
I sought for the reality
I'd heard confers pure bliss.

The many names of God I learned,
And one by one I tried
To shift my burdens onto them,
But seeking them outside.

My next discovery was that God
Inside of me did dwell,
But in which part of me He lived
I simply could not tell.

So finally I just gave up
And begged that He seek me,
And show me how to change my life
To live successfully.

And then I read of Baba,
Who must have heard me call,
So off I went to visit him
And at his feet to fall.

Since then he's shown me clearly
That I must do my part
And enter every phase of life,
Knowing God is in my heart.

So now I'll try to live my life,
Not with my human will,
But seeking inner guidance
When my busy mind is still.

How often when I stumble,
If the name of God I sing,
He and I together
Can handle anything.

Chapter 39

Go and Do!

Despite my busy life and heavy travel schedule, to my genuine surprise and relief the book was almost finished within the year as Baba had directed, except for two or three chapters—including this one—which had to be written after we returned home from seeing him. Admittedly, it was written in fits and starts whenever I had time, but only on those occasions when it flowed freely from Baba's pen, for it appeared to have its own timing and sequence. So, my husband, Sidney, and I planned to follow Baba's instructions and take the manuscript to him for his blessing in time for the opening of the new hospital on November 22, 1991, the day before his next birthday.

It was quite a feat to prepare for this visit, for I had only one week in which to get ready, having just returned from Europe where I had been giving talks and workshops. But as usual—when we follow the inner direction and relax and let the Higher Self direct the process—everything fell into place like clockwork. We arrived at the ashram just in time for the opening ceremony.

This time we had arranged to be at the ashram for only ten days, so as soon as the festivities were over I decided to carry the bulky manuscript with me to the daily *darshans* to avoid being caught without it whenever Baba was ready to accept it. What I did not know was that Baba would test me to the hilt during this visit. I had written a book about the monkey mind, but would I be able to practice what I preached right under Baba's nose in the midst of the huge crowds of other devotees and still keep my own monkey mind under control?

For days Baba sent not so much as a glance in my direction, while others—including my own husband—were granted interviews; saris were given to some of the ladies, and *padnamaskar* (touching his feet) and various other acknowledgments were given to many of our friends. I was forced to examine my reactions more stringently than ever before and with complete honesty. What were my feelings right now? Baba had told me on our last visit that I was writing another book even though, until then, I had no intention of doing so. Now, having written it and brought it to him for his blessing as he had requested, how did I feel to have him completely ignore me? First, I questioned whether I was feeling envious or jealous of any of those on whom he was showering favors. But to that question I could honestly say "No," for I knew very well that I only ever want what is intended for me, which may not be what someone else needs. I was certain that I did not begrudge those what Baba chose to give them, in fact I was genuinely happy for them, for I knew the thrill of receiving something from Baba.

Then it suddenly became clear to me that what was bothering me was not knowing what I had done wrong or where I had failed. Perhaps the book was not as Baba wished, but then I remembered the time I had taken a previous manuscript to him. When he accepted it I asked him if it was the way he wanted it. He bored into me with his penetrating eyes and, pointing a finger at me, said, "Incorrect. Is it the way *you* think it should be?" as he looked deep inside to the real Me. In other words, he was warning me not to rely on his outer physical form to give me the answers I sought, but to consult my inner Self.

So, as that was not the problem, what was it? My monkey mind would not let go, so the questions persisted nonstop. After a great deal more soul-searching, quite suddenly and without warning, I found myself transported back in memory to my childhood. I immediately recognized the feelings I was having, which were so familiar yet so illusive. They were the very ones I had suffered throughout my childhood. Whenever my mother punished me I was never told what I had done to merit it, what I had done wrong, failed to execute perfectly, or what I had omitted doing. Not only did she refrain from telling me the reason for the punishment, but if I ever asked her, she would accuse me of being impertinent; a deadly sin in her estimation! Although I had not the slightest idea of the meaning of that word I was punished again for the added indiscretion. So I learned never to ask again, which left many questions chasing around in my head. Consequently, I moved through childhood as if I were walking on thin ice or eggshells, never feeling secure and momentarily expecting to be punished again for committing an unknown error.

It was indeed a shock to discover that this little girl was still active inside me and still reacting as she had done all those many years ago. I no longer wanted any part of her. She was a perfect nuisance (a phrase my mother would often use about me when I was a child). Where was the Self-confidence that Baba says we must develop now that he is here to teach us who we really are? It was certainly not part of this insecure and confused little girl. I was also shocked that after working for so long to uncover the hidden parts of myself, I had remained unaware of this major one. How did it escape my attention for so long? Then I knew, without a shadow of a doubt, that this was the perfect time and that Baba, who is so aware of correct timing, was giving me an opportunity to bring her up into the light of consciousness while I was close to his wonderfully loving and supportive energy. But now that I had done so, what was to be done with her?

In answer to that question, quite spontaneously, I gathered her up (figuratively speaking) and handed her over to Baba with the earnest plea to help me detach myself from her and the continuing influence she had on my life, especially on my relationship with him, since Baba symbolizes the loving mother I and many others never had. For, in addition to representing in human form the God-self we all really are, Baba also symbolizes the supremely loving mother/father figure for each of us. But if we project onto him an image similar to our early view of either of our parents, he will hold up a mirror to show us that we are reacting to him exactly as we used to do to one or the other of them. It was a wonderful relief to be free from this intrusive aspect of my childhood. What a beautiful gift Baba gave me! He will also give similar gifts to anyone else who responds to this pattern, if they ask.

However, the testing was by no means over yet. My questions continued unabated. Could I remain unruffled if Baba did not call us? In that case I would have to return home without receiving his blessing on the book. And how would I feel about having it published without his sanction? Then I recalled that Sidney had told me that when he had been included in an earlier interview and had asked if he should call me, Baba had replied, "Not now. I will see her later." So I must trust that he would keep his promise.

The days flew by and our stay was nearing the end. On our last day, knowing that we planned to leave after the morning *darshan*—which would be my last chance to give the book to Baba—Mrs. Hejmadi, the head volunteer, insisted that I be seated in a very prominent place where Baba could not miss seeing me. Overriding my objections, she assured me that it was customary for devotees to let him know that they were leaving. So I sat where she placed me, with the manuscript tucked out of sight by my side. As soon as Baba appeared he walked directly over to where I was sitting and, with a sweet smile as if he were seeing me for the first time said, "Yes, Mrs. Krystal and where is the book?" When I held it up toward him he smiled again and said, "Very, very happy." Then, turning quickly, he continued on his way along the long lines of devotees awaiting his *darshan*. At the end of the *darshan* he called a large group for an interview, which was the signal for most of the crowd to leave the area.

What should I do now? Here, my monkey mind took over again. Instead of taking the small plane to Bangalore in order to avoid the three-and-a-half-hour drive over rutted roads, we could ride back in the taxi we had ordered to take our luggage. If we left after the afternoon *darshan*, I would have one more chance to give Baba the book. I was still considering these alternative plans when Mrs. Hejmadi hurried up to tell me not to leave. She informed me that the big group that Baba had taken in for an interview were the doctors and nurses who had been working at the new hospital. She explained that on a few occasions Baba had been known to call a second group, and there was still a chance that he would call us after they all came out. So I remained seated while many others were leaving to take a break and have something to eat. The war of nerves was on again! As I sat there I tried to accept as calmly as possible whatever was going to happen and silently repeated, "Surrender, Trust, and Accept" like a mantra.

After what felt like hours had elapsed, people began to trickle back again to await the start of *bhajans*. Finally, the medical group filed out just as *bhajans* were about to begin, and I saw Sidney get up to leave the veranda, obviously concluding that Baba was not going to see us. My heart sank, but at that very moment Baba emerged and, noticing that Sidney was leaving, quickly called him to come back and to signal to me to join him.

A wave of relief swept over me as I hurried along with Mrs. Hejmadi as fast as I could across the intervening space, which seemed more like several miles instead of yards, only to have Baba chide me for moving too slowly and urge me to hurry. Then, right there, standing on the veranda, he asked for the book, which I thankfully handed to him. He then proceeded to ask me its title and insisted that I repeat it three times, urging me to speak more loudly each time. Next, he asked me the titles of the three previous books, again having me repeat each one three times and insisting that I speak even more loudly so that everyone around could hear. What better way to instill Self-confidence into someone who had always been so sadly lacking it?

As this little scene was being played out, I concluded that this was our interview: right out here in the open in full view of thousands of visitors. So, when Baba waved us both into the interview room I was genuinely surprised. Seeing me hesitate he again exhorted me to hurry. The interview that followed was one of the strangest I have ever experienced. In the first place, the *bhajans* had already started and were so loud that it was difficult to hear Baba's soft voice when he spoke to us. Added to that, when it came time to ask the questions I had written out on a piece of paper, I simply could not find my reading glasses in my handbag, and I needed them to be able to read the questions. After searching in vain, I started to hand the list to Sidney and asked him to read them aloud for me. But Baba snatched the list out of my hand and read the questions, murmuring the answers in such a soft voice that I could neither hear nor understand what he said, especially with the sound of the *bhajan* singing ringing in my ears. After a brief discussion about the book, my itinerary for 1992, the family, and other matters, Baba turned suddenly, looked at me piercingly, and commanded in a loud and forceful voice, "Go and do!"

It so happened that just a few days before this interview I had been talking to a German devotee who mentioned that one of the songs that were sung at a Sai conference held in Hamburg two years earlier was based on something Baba had said to him in an interview, which was, "Go and do." Ever since I first heard it sung it has been one of my favorites. Now, here was Baba giving me the same command to "Go and do." With those words echoing in my head, Baba brought the interview to an end, but first he granted me *padnamaskar*. Then, bringing his hand down firmly on each of our heads, he gave us *vibhuti* and dismissed us. In a daze I walked back to my place, weaving my way between the lines of seated devotees stretching out in all directions. As usual in an interview my mind had been a complete blank and it still was, but this time even more so. After *bhajans* ended, we hurried back to our room to pack the last few items before leaving for Bangalore and our flight home.

It was not until after I had arrived home and was able to look back at the recent visit and gain more perspective on all that had taken place that even more of Baba's message became clear. Because it may be applicable to many others, I have decided to share the insights I received. It has been fascinating to have some people who have come to work with me, without knowing about my recent experience and the resulting insights, tell me that they have become aware that they are still behaving as they did when they were children! And some devotees have even said they have begun to notice that they project on to Baba the memory of their mother's or father's attitude toward them and often react to him as they used to react to their parents.

So the image of the bewildered little girl who never knew why she was being punished can now help others whose childhood behavior is lying in wait, ready to spring up like a jack-in-the-box when the present circumstances trigger it into action. Obviously, not all these childish parts in others are necessarily like the one I discovered hiding inside me. The characteristics depend upon the internalized image of the parent and the reactions to it that each adult has retained from childhood.

Another insight that burst upon me one day was the reason Baba kept telling me to hurry when I was already walking or speaking as fast as I could, and also why he insisted that I speak louder. Those too were typical of my mother's treatment of me, so again he was assuming her behavior so that I could see how I was still reacting as I had done as a child. I also began to realize that because I never knew what I had done to warrant the punishment meted out to me, I thought everyone else was right and more knowledgeable than me, so everyone became an authority figure in my eyes. No wonder I have always felt more at ease when I stayed silently in the background and out of sight, a habit Baba has continuously helped me to break by constantly forcing me out of the shadows and into the spotlight, albeit to my extreme discomfort. This last interview was a good example of this. How patient he is with all of us and how slow some of us are to get the point of what he is teaching, and how reluctant we often are to let go of these old patterns and admit to what he is always telling us: that we are all God and not inadequate children.

So we must detach ourselves from anyone or anything that has the power to prevent us from relying on our real Self and develop Self-confidence so that we do not need anyone else's approval of who we are or what we do. That includes seeking Baba's approval, too. For he obviously wants each of us to take the responsibility for putting his teachings into practice in our lives with Self-confidence, instead of forgetting who we really are and allowing our monkey mind to prevent us from being directed from within. Then we can do as Baba directs: "Be your own guru; your own teacher. You have the lamp within you. Light it and march on without fear."

So let us heed Baba's clarion call and have the courage to "Go and do."

Tread lightly on the days stretched out ahead of you.
Leave as little mark as possible on your own ego self.
Let the light from within enclose each day.
And when it is finished, blow it away as you would a soap
    bubble
And move forward unencumbered by old memories, mistakes,
    and successes.
This is the way to peace.

Glossary of Indian Words

ahimsa: the principle of non-violence.

amrita: Divine nectar.

ashram: the hermitage or abode of a spiritual teacher where devotees may gather to receive his or her blessing.

Atma: Divine essence in all beings. The highest principle of life.

bhajans: devotional songs similar to hymns.

darshan: the blessing received at the sight of a master.

dharma: righteous divine order and ethical precepts for living.

dharmic: putting Truth into practice.

gunas: the three attributes inherent in all beings, sathwa, rajas and tamas.

japamala: a string of prayer beads similar to a rosary usually containing 108 beads for counting prayers.

Kali Yuga: the last of a cycle of four ages or yugas. The present Kali Yuga is the most negative on an individual, as well as world level.

padnamaskar: the act of touching the feet of the guru or teacher. In other words, the ego bows at the feet of the guru.

prema: unconditional love for all, free from attachment.

rajasic: the quality of being passionate and active when applied to behavior and food that incites.

sadhu: a holy person or advanced soul dedicated to the inner path.

sathwic: calm, unruffled and full of peace.

sathya: pure and eternal Truth.

shanti: peace and peace of mind.

ttamasic: quality of being sluggish, heavy, and lazy in acts and food.

vibhuti: sacred ash used for healing.

Yagna: a spiritual exercise or offering as devotion.

Phyllis Krystal is a psychotherapist. She was born in England but lives and works in California where she has developed her own techniques of psychotherapy. For over forty years, she has been developing a counseling method using symbols and visualization techniques that help people detach from external authority figures and patterns in order to rely on their own Higher Consciousness as guide and teacher. To teach the method, Krystal gives lectures and seminars in the USA and many other countries. She is a devotee of Sathya Sai Baba, a world teacher living in India whose teachings and personal influence have been an inspiration. She is the author of *Cutting the Ties that Bind*, *Cutting More Ties that Bind*, and *Sai Baba: The Ultimate Experience*, also published by Samuel Weiser, Inc.